JUST PLANE CRAZY

To order additional copies of *Just Plane Crazy*,
by Melanie Scherencel Bockmann,
call 1-800-765-6955.

Visit us at **www.reviewandherald.com**
for information on other
Review and Herald® products.

A Guide
True Story
Book

JUST PLANE CRAZY

Melanie Scherencel
BOCKMANN

REVIEW AND HERALD® PUBLISHING ASSOCIATION
HAGERSTOWN, MD 21740

The Review and Herald® Publishing Association publishes
biblically-based materials for spiritual, physical, and mental growth and
Christian discipleship.

The author assumes full responsibility for the accuracy of all facts and
quotations as cited in this book.

This book was
Edited by Penny Estes Wheeler
Cover design by Trent Truman
Interior design by Candy Harvey
Electronic makeup by Shirley M. Bolivar
Cover art by Macky Pamintuan
Typeset: Goudy 13/16

PRINTED IN U.S.A.

10 09 08 07 06   5 4 3 2 1

R&H Cataloging Service
Bockmann, Melanie Scherencel, 1974-   .
    Just plane crazy.

1. Brothers and sisters—stories
    I. Title.

        306.8753

ISBN 10: 0-8280-1919-3
ISBN 13: 978-0-8280-1919-4

To my husband, Tim . . .

*You are my love, my inspiration, my courageous
adventurer. I'll follow you anywhere.*

To Jagger . . .

*You are the apple of my eye. Don't ever forget that
sometimes the biggest things
come in the smallest packages. Wait and see.*

To Tyson . . .

*From the moment you were born,
I recognized your amazing inner strength.
You were predestined to be a warrior of light,
and I'm proud to be your mom.*

To Jef . . .

*You have the biggest dreams of anyone I have ever met,
and I can't wait to see what great things you accomplish.
Maybe someday I'll be writing about your adventures.*

To Beau . . .

*Sometimes when I straighten your bowtie
before a special event, watch football with you on Sunday
afternoon, or listen while you confide in me,
it hits me how lucky I am.
Thanks for letting me be a part of your life.*

Chapter 1

Rick squinted at the instrument panel of the Cessna 185 airplane, then cautiously tapped his finger on the steamy fuel gauge. Just as he expected, the needle tipped toward empty. He shivered. The armed rebel hovered so closely that Rick hardly dared move, much less say anything. But keeping his eyes forward, he gathered his nerve and spoke.

"Our fuel reserves are low," Rick said loudly over the rumbling of the airplane engine. Carefully avoiding eye contact, he swallowed and continued. "The plane will not fly much longer. I warned you when you forced yourself aboard this mission plane that I did not have enough fuel for a long flight."

"We must reach our destination. We need the supplies in this airplane for our cause." The lone hijacker gripped the gun in his hands so tightly that his knuckles turned white.

Rick looked out the vibrating window, praying as he gazed down over the canopy of unfamiliar jungle territory below. It would be a matter of minutes before the engine stalled and they'd be swallowed into the abyss of trees, never to be heard from again. Drops of sweat beaded on his forehead as he tried to think of a way to escape the impending crash.

The hijacker shoved the gun into Rick's face. "Just do as you're told," he demanded, the gun barrel dangerously close to Rick's right eye.

"OK! Stop! Time out. Be careful with that stick," Rick told his little brother, Tim. He grabbed it and held it while he talked. "Mom specifically said you could use a stick only if you didn't poke my eyes out with it."

"I am being careful." Tim jerked the stick out of Rick's hand and repositioned it as he adjusted the camouflage bandana that had fallen over his eyes. "And you're the victim. Victims don't get to make the demands. Now, act scared of me."

"I don't have to *act* scared," Rick countered, holding a protective hand between himself and the stick's point. "I'm terrified that you're going to skewer my eyeball with that thing."

Keenly aware of the dangerous weapon the hijacker insisted on keeping near his face, Rick scanned the thick umbrella of trees below. There was no place to land. Soon they'd be at the mercy of gravity. Then, suddenly, the idea for escape that Rick had begged God for came to him. Calculating just the right moment, in one swift move he knocked the gun from the hijacker's hands, grabbed his parachute, and jumped out of the plane. Wind whipped in his ears while he strapped on the parachute and fumbled *frantically for the ripcord. The parachute opened, jerking him upward before dropping him slowly to the jungle floor. At that same moment the plane stalled and fell, crashing down through the trees. When the confetti of shredded leaves and dirt settled, Rick grimaced at the wreckage. The Cessna 185 was a total loss, and the hijacker had perished. Rick must seek survival alone in the jungle.*

"Wait a minute. I don't want to perish," Tim complained. "I want to keep playing."

Rick sighed and shook his head.

Miraculously, the hijacker survived the plane crash, and continued to test the patience of the courageous mission pilot. Rick tried to pull himself from the tangled parachute, but was unsuccessful. His captor emerged from the wreckage and stood over him.

"You thought you could escape, did you?" The rebel gave a taunting laugh. "Well, mission pilot, even if you survived me, you can not survive the poisonous snakes and wild animals of the Peruvian jungle."

Without warning, other smaller rebels emerged from the bush and attacked Rick. He lay helpless, at their mercy.

"Hey, this isn't fair," Rick said, pushing Tim, his baby brother Chris, and baby sister Laurie off of him as they giggled and tickled him with their fingers. "There's only one of me and three of you."

It was no use. The native rebels subdued him with torture tactics, and soon held him captive in a bamboo jail cell while they celebrated his capture. Rick fearlessly watched them from inside his makeshift prison, certain that this was part of God's plan to turn the rebels into soldiers in the kingdom of light.

The village warrior princess came out of her hut. "Are you hungry?" she inquired. Her voice was kind.

"What?" Rick asked.

"I said, 'are you hungry?'" Mom repeated. "Come out from under the coffee table and wash your hands for dinner."

"Aw, Mom, not yet," Tim complained. "Me and Chris and Laurie haven't even been converted yet."

"Excuse me," Mom said, picking Chris up and tickling under his arms. "The village warrior princess has spoken. No uncivilized behavior tonight. And if someone could please salvage my dining-room chairs from the plane wreckage in the living room and bring them back to the table, I'd appreciate it."

"Can we play again after dinner?" Tim begged Rick, his eyes dancing with excitement as he pulled his chair back into the dining room. "Next time, can I be the missionary pilot, and you and Laurie and Chris be the infidels?"

"We'll see," Rick said, ruffling Tim's hair. "But go get your hands washed for dinner."

Just then, Dad walked in the front door. "Smells good in here," he said, picking Laurie up in his arms and giving Mom a quick kiss. "Did you all have fun on your first day of summer vacation?"

"Yeah," Rick shrugged as he pulled up his chair

next to the dinner table. "If you call being hijacked by native rebels, parachuting an escape, and crashing your plane in the jungle fun." Looking across the table at Tim, he made a silly face.

"Ah, I see you've been entertaining your little brothers and sister for your mom again." Dad's eyes twinkled. "They never get tired of playing missionary bush pilot with their big brother, do they?"

With a smile, Rick shook his head as he scooted his chair in toward the table and took off his hat for prayer.

Mom buckled Laurie into her high chair, and then sat down at the table with everyone else. Dad smiled and winked at her, and then took her hand as he bowed his head for the blessing.

"Speaking of missionary bush pilots, I got a letter today," Dad said when he'd finished the prayer. He dished out a helping of rice casserole then passed it on to Rick. "Remember your mom's and my friends who are missionaries in Peru? They sent us another letter. I'll read it to you kids during worship tonight. Oh, and Rick," he added, "something came for you, too."

Rick swallowed a forkful of salad. "For me? What is it?"

"It's that flight magazine you ordered. It looks pretty cool, and it even has an airplane buying guide in it with all kinds of specifications and things."

Rick knew he had to choke down a few more bites of dinner to satisfy his mom before he could check out his new magazine. He finished as fast as he could, and then wadded up his napkin into a ball before picking up his empty dinner plate and juice glass.

"Dad, where's that magazine?" Rick asked as he rinsed his plate at the kitchen sink.

"It's on the coffee table," Dad said, wiping his mouth. "Did you boys practice your trumpets today?"

"For half an hour," Rick answered, picking up his new magazine and heading up to his room.

This is incredible, Rick thought. He was sprawled out on his bed, feet dangling over the edge, as he looked at the featured planes. Each picture had a full view, and a cutaway view so that he could see the interiors of the planes. He thumbed through the pages until he came to a picture of a yellow Super Cub airplane. With an open mouth, Rick stared at the beautiful, sleek lines and black trim.

"The legend lives," Rick whispered to himself, thinking of the pictures in his airplane encyclopedia. "Oh, man, here's one for sale that looks practically new."

It would be a perfect plane for a missionary bush pilot: the right amount of cargo space, and two seats—one for him and one for his best friend, Marcus. Not fast, but light and agile. It had a fully enclosed engine compartment and a powerful engine for short takeoff and landing. It had to be the most awesome thing he'd ever seen. He picked up the phone and dialed Marcus' number.

"Hello—"

"Hey, it's me," Rick said, barely waiting for Marcus to get out the word. "Guess what came in the mail today?"

"An elephant?" Marcus guessed wryly.

"No, better," Rick laughed. "It's this magazine I've been waiting for. I'll show you tomorrow. You've got to come over and see this."

"All right." Marcus sounded dejected. "But I've got to get my room clean first."

"Why?" Rick moaned. "It's the first day of summer vacation."

"I know," Marcus sighed, "but Mom told me she can't remember the color of my carpet because of all my stuff. She says I'm a prisoner until I get my room as clean as my sister's room is."

Rick slapped his own forehead with the palm of his hand and dropped to the carpet. "No! Your sister is a pathological neat freak. She might as well have said you're grounded forever."

"I know," Marcus said. "Mom's unmerciful."

"Well hurry up," Rick demanded. "And get over here as early as possible."

"I'll try." He didn't sound hopeful. "But if you don't see me right away, it's because I've been detained by enemy forces." He paused. Another loud sigh. "Oh, guess what? Somebody's moving in across the street from your house. I just saw the moving truck today."

"Any kids our age?" Rick asked, scrambling up off the floor to look out the window.

"I don't know," Marcus said. "I saw the guys unload a bike, so maybe. We'll have to check it out. Hang on a second. My sister is saying something to me."

Rick heard Marcus cover the phone with his hand and muffled conversation before his friend came back to the line. "I have to go. Carlie wants to use the phone, and she won't leave me alone until I let her. If only my sister would use her powers for good, and not evil."

Rick smiled. He could hear his mom calling him downstairs for their evening worship time. "I have to go anyway. See you in the morning?"

"I hope so."

Rick hung up the phone and peeked out his bedroom window once more at the house across the street. Sure enough, its lights were on, and through the window Rick could see moving boxes piled high in the living room.

"Rick, are you coming?" Dad called.

Rick sauntered down the stairs and plopped himself on the couch, pulling his little brother Chris onto his lap. Mom, Tim, and Laurie were snuggled in on the loveseat, and Dad was in the recliner with his reading glasses on.

Closing his eyes, Rick let his imagination travel to Peru as he listened to Dad read. The stories that came in the letters from the missionaries always left his imagination reeling. He could almost hear the screams of hungry jungle animals, and the high whine of bloodsucking insects buzzing in his ears. He imagined hostile men and women trying their best to stop the work of the missionaries, and the miraculous circumstances surrounding rescues from plane crashes and other situations where God intervened against all opposing odds. Rick knew one thing for sure: a missionary couldn't be a wimp. They had to be ready for anything. And they had to be filled with the Holy Spirit and have faith in God as strong as iron. Rick could imagine himself flying low over the jungles in his shiny, yellow Super Cub, hauling medical supplies to distant villages, living on the cutting edge of faith, and resisting evil forces by fulfilling assignments for God.

Everyone sat in silence for a moment when Dad finished reading the letter.

"It sounds like they need supplies," Mom said, a thoughtful look on her face. "Especially diapers and other things for babies. We should package some to send for the mission."

To close their worship time, the family held hands in a circle, and each person took a turn praying. Rick prayed especially for the missionaries, asking for protection for them, and for the power of the Holy Spirit in their work.

After helping Dad brush the little kids' teeth and get them into their pajamas, then hugging Mom goodnight, Rick climbed into his bed and stared upward. Tim's upside-down face soon appeared over the edge of the top bunk. "Yes?" Rick asked, stretching his arms and folding them behind his head.

"Well, I just thought I'd tell you that I've decided I want to be a missionary," Tim said. "Not like what you played with me today. I mean for real."

Rick smiled in the near-darkness. "Yeah, me too," he whispered. He saw Tim pull himself back up onto the top bunk and felt the bed wiggle as his little brother made himself comfortable on his pillow and pulled the light blanket up to his neck. Soon Rick heard his steady breathing. As for him, he couldn't sleep. He couldn't stop thinking about the letter his dad had read, and a ball of excitement in the pit of his stomach kept him awake. An idea was forming in Rick's mind. Why wait? He could start raising money to buy that Super Cub right now—this summer. Then, when he received his pilot's license, he'd already have a plane and could get started as a missionary bush pilot sooner.

Rick tried to close his eyes and rest to the sound of the Northwest summer rain falling outside. But with all of the ideas beginning to spin around in his head, he didn't see how he'd be able to sleep at all.

Chapter 2

I spent the morning cleaning my room so that I could look at a picture of an airplane?" Marcus said, unimpressed by Rick's magazine.

"Hey, not just any airplane. *I'd* even clean your room for this," Rick said, flipping the pages to the picture of the Super Cub. "Listen. You know how we always talk about being mission pilots?"

"Yeah," Marcus said, eyeing the photograph. "Keep talking."

"Just take a look at the specs for this airplane." Rick pointed at each feature as he talked. "It's perfect. Two seats, cargo space for medical supplies, books, food, and whatever else. It's light and easy to fly, and it can probably even be fitted with pontoons to land in the water, so it could be taken anywhere. Perfect for a team of mission pilots, right?"

"Well, yeah, it would be great—" Marcus started to say, but Rick interrupted him before he could say something too practical.

"What if—just listen—what if we started raising the money now to buy the Super Cub?" Rick thumped his hand on the picture. "By the time we're old enough to get our pilots' licenses—which really isn't *that* long, if you think about it—we'd have enough money saved up to buy the plane."

Rick waited impatiently for the thought to sink in, and after a few seconds, Marcus started nodding.

"Yeah; I mean, yeah, why not?" Marcus said, his voice rising with excitement. "We could start pooling our allowances, maybe even open a savings account and earn interest on the money." Rick could tell by the look in Marcus' eyes that he was sold on the idea.

"Yes," Rick said. "Let's do it."

"Yes, let's do it," said a muffled voice from under the bed.

Rick and Marcus looked at each other, then knelt down and lifted up the edge of the comforter for a look.

"Tim. What are you doing under there?" Rick demanded. "This was a private meeting."

Tim bumped his head on his way out from under the bed. He stood looking at Rick and Marcus, rubbing his head furiously with the palm of his hand. "Ouch."

Rick tried to be patient with him. "Tim, you're going to have to go on out so that Marcus and I can talk. I'll play with you later, but right now, Marcus and I have a lot of planning to do."

Rick and Marcus pulled the money out of their wallets, and pooled it in a pile on the floor. Marcus started counting it while Rick got out his calculator.

Tim didn't budge. "But I want to go in the plane, too."

"You can't," Rick said, nudging him toward the door. "Marcus and I aren't pretending. This isn't the same as when I play with you. We're serious. Besides, it's a Super Cub with two seats. There isn't room for anyone else."

Marcus sighed as he looked up. "Well, we have a grand total of $67.14. That's pathetic."

"That's all you have with both of you?" Tim laughed. "I have more than that by myself because I don't spend it on stuff like you do. I've saved about $100. You can even ask Mom."

"Out, Tim," Rick demanded, losing his patience. "It's not nice to brag." He shook his head as he punched figures into his calculator. "This *is* a slow start," he complained to Marcus. "And by my estimates, with our future allowances combined, it will take us 63.1 years to raise enough cash to buy the plane."

Tim wedged himself in between the two bigger boys and looked at the picture of the Super Cub. "I'm not heavy," he said, pointing to the cutaway view of the airplane's cargo area. "Why can't you just put a seat for me right there?"

"Tim, go *out* and let us talk," Rick sighed. "You won't fit, and besides, I don't want my little brother tagging along on dangerous missions."

"Yeah," Marcus added, pointing at Rick with his thumb. "What he said."

"I won't get in the way," Tim resisted.

"You're in the way right now. Mom!" Rick called, standing up and trying to herd Tim toward the bedroom door.

Rick and Marcus pulled on him from every direction, but Tim caught the bedpost and held on for dear life.

"Let go," Rick hissed as he wrestled against Tim's wiry little body.

Tim clung to the bed frame in desperation. "Please let me stay. You—can—you can have my *allowance*."

Rick and Marcus stopped tugging and looked at each other, then down at Tim's hopeful face.

"Did you say you've saved about $100?" Rick asked slowly.

Tim nodded.

"On second thought, he *might* fit." Marcus shrugged. "He wouldn't weigh any more than the cargo."

"True," Rick said, mentally calculating the maximum load capacity. "We could put a small seat in for him in the cargo area. There'd probably be enough oxygen in there for him to survive."

"And, we might be able to use him as a diversion tactic in case of an emergency," Marcus noted. "You know, he could distract any officials who might try to stop us while we make a clean getaway."

Rick and Marcus released their grip on Tim's legs, and Tim plopped onto the floor. Just then Mom peeked her head in the door. "Is everything all right?

Tim, are you pestering your big brother again?"

Tim looked up at Rick with pleading eyes.

Rick thought fast before he answered. "It's OK, Mom. He can stay in here with us if he wants."

Mom seemed puzzled as she looked at each of them, and then shook her head. "I thought for sure you'd called . . ." The boys could hear her voice trailing off as she walked down the hall away from their bedroom.

"OK, you're in," Rick said finally.

"Thanks, guys," Tim said, adjusting his twisted clothing. "I'll go get my allowance out of my piggy bank."

"But you're going to have to be a silent partner," Rick whispered.

"I have to be quiet?" Tim looked incredulous.

Marcus laughed. "'Silent partner' means you'll contribute your allowance, but Rick and I will have to make all of the important decisions."

Tim seemed satisfied as long as he was part of the plan. He dug around in a drawer until he found a plastic jar, opened it, and emptied his savings out onto the pile.

Marcus frowned.

"We're still a long way from where we need to be."

"Yeah," Rick replied. "We're going to have to ask for an advance on birthday money and Christmas money and college money. Or we could take out a loan from our parents."

Marcus stood up. "Right, like that's going to

work. Think it over and let me know what you come up with. I'll come by later and we can do some brainstorming."

"Sounds good," Rick said.

When Dad came home that evening, Rick told him about their plan and asked him if he had any ideas on how to get the money. "Maybe you'd like to make a sizeable donation to the cause?" Rick asked hopefully. "Or maybe a moderate loan?"

Dad looked at the pictures of the Super Cub thoughtfully.

"Well, Rick, I think that it's a fantastic plan to start saving money now." Dad looked impressed. "I'm glad that you're setting honorable goals and working toward them. However," he continued, "instead of borrowing or begging for the money for your airplane, I think you'd appreciate your achievement more if you earn the money the old-fashioned way."

"The old-fashioned way?" Marcus repeated, saying the words as if they had a strange taste. He and Rick were walking down the sidewalk. "What's that supposed to mean?"

"I don't know." They'd stopped a little past the house that housed their new neighbors, and Rick poked the ground with a stick. "What ideas did you come up with?"

"I tried to get my mom to give me a raise on my allowance. She just said that she'd pay good money to see my bedroom stay clean." Marcus made a face.

"Well, we all know *that* option's out."

Both boys were quiet as they shuffled down the street, deep in thought. The sun had finally come out, and the water on the sidewalks evaporated slowly, along with the boys' enthusiasm.

"Hey, look," Marcus pointed. "Mr. Bushnell is having a garage sale. Let's go see what he's selling."

Rick and Marcus said hello to Mr. Bushnell, their neighbor, and then wandered from table to table, looking at the sale items.

"What's this?" Rick asked, picking up some metal devices.

"Animal traps," Mr. Bushnell said.

"You mean like old-fashioned trappers used to get furs to sell?" Rick turned the metal trap in his hand and tried to pull it apart.

"Yep," Mr. Bushnell said.

"Hey." Marcus stopped and grabbed Rick's shoulder. "Would that be an 'old fashioned' way to get money? You know, selling fox furs to rich people?"

"I'm not sure my parents will like it if I take up hunting." Rick wrinkled his forehead and looked at Marcus.

"Yeah, mine either." Marcus was quiet for a moment, and then he brightened. "Except that we're doing it for a good cause. I mean, we're raising the money to be missionary pilots, right? Besides that, I distinctly remember reading in the Bible that Nimrod was a mighty hunter before the Lord. If they have any objections, we'll tell them we're following Nimrod's example."

"I think you actually have to catch something before you qualify as 'mighty,' but I also think you're on to something." Rick picked up the traps in his arms and went to negotiate a price with Mr. Bushnell, using part of their airplane money as an investment. Mr. Bushnell showed the boys how to set and bait the traps.

"You probably should set them out in the woods, away from the houses," Mr. Bushnell said. "You might be able to catch yourselves a rabbit." Rick smiled politely at Mr. Bushnell's suggestion. He thought it would be rude to tell him that their aims were much higher—to catch foxes and sell the fur.

Mr. Bushnell waved as they left. "Good luck."

Just then Rick heard a familiar whistle. "Oh, no. It's my mom. I've got to go home."

"Oh, man." Marcus' shoulders sagged, and he looked at the traps with big eyes. "You mean that we've gotta wait until tomorrow?"

"If I don't go in now, there won't *be* a tomorrow for me. I'll get into trouble and be stuck weeding flowerbeds or something." Rick watched Marcus' face and hoped he'd understand.

Marcus nodded. "OK. Let's meet first thing in the morning. See you tomorrow."

Rick watched Marcus walk down Dogwood Drive before turning to go inside. Out of the corner of his eye, he saw something move. Stacking the traps inside the garage, Rick studied the house across the street. He thought he saw a boy's face in the window, but when he waved, the face disappeared and the curtains fell back into place.

Well, if that was the new neighbor kid, he isn't very friendly, Rick thought. *Or maybe he's just shy.* He opened the front door and walked inside, but he had the uncomfortable feeling that the face in the window across the street was still watching him.

Chapter 3

The cool morning air put goose bumps on Rick's arms as he carried the metal traps deep into the forested area to where a grove of saplings grew. Tim, who'd stubbornly refused to be left behind, trudged along beside him carrying the bait. Marcus had promised to meet them there the second his mom let him out of the house.

Through the trees, Rick could hear the low buzz of an airplane coming in to land at the small airport beyond the woods. With his love of flying, Rick had all of the local pilots and their airplanes memorized. Instantly, he knew who it was as the plane stormed overhead. "Look!" he shouted to Tim over the noise as the red-nosed aircraft buzzed the field before landing. "It's the P-51 Mustang." He and Tim shielded their eyes against the sun and watched the plane disappear over the edge of the treetops.

"It's awesome," Tim yelled as he looked up at the sky.

One memorable day, Mr. Schwartz, the proud owner of the P-51 Mustang, had let Rick look all around inside his plane. Rick had been talking to Jim and Rob, the mechanics at the airplane hangar, and Mr. Schwartz, in a thick accent, had been more than happy to answer all of Rick's questions.

"Ah," Mr. Schwartz had said, "someday you fly, yah?"

"Yeah," he told Mr. Schwartz. "Someday I'll fly. You bet."

Rick often dreamed of flying above the clouds, and on that day as he'd run his hands over the smooth metal belly of the P-51 Mustang, he knew that the time would come when he'd own his own plane. Since then, every time Rick saw an airplane suspended in the sky, his determination became stronger.

"It's about time you guys got here."

A voice shattered 'Rick's daydream. Marcus jumped down off of the tree stump where he'd been sitting, and threw his hands in the air. "I thought I was going to be middle-aged with a wife and kids by the time you showed up."

Rick dropped the metal traps on the ground. "Your hairline is receding a little."

"Whatever," Marcus answered, but his hand flew up to his forehead. "Let's get these things set up. Where should we put them?"

Tim sat down on a log, cradling the bait in his lap while he watched the older boys scour the area for a good trap site. "How about under that bush?" Tim suggested.

"Well, no, I don't think that will work," Rick said, looking around. "We need to find a worn area—like a trail. I read that foxes will usually choose the path of least resistance, so we can't put the traps near any tall grass or bushes. How about over there?"

A small animal trail curved off the main path through the trees, and Marcus chewed his lower lip while he nodded. "Yep, perfect."

Rick and Marcus positioned the first trap in the path and pounded the stake into the ground with a mallet. Marcus pulled the lever down while Rick gritted his teeth and pulled the metal claws apart.

"Snap the centerpiece into place," Rick commanded slowly, "and set the spring."

"Don't let go, or Marcus' hand will be chopped off," Tim offered cheerfully from the sidelines.

"Thanks," Rick said between clenched teeth.

Marcus reached into the center and pushed the spring-loaded paddle into place. Rick gradually let go and fully removed his hands when he saw that the spring held.

"Wait," Marcus said, scratching his head. "Shouldn't we have baited it?"

"Oh, yeah," Rick agreed. "Tim, bring us the bait."

"What did you bring for a lure? Shellfish paste? Castor oil and musk drops? Mr. Bushnell said that aged intestines work well. Come, bait-keeper, show me what you have." Marcus turned to look at Tim, and his mouth dropped open. He stood dumbfounded for a heartbeat before he spoke in a strained voice. "Rick, whatever you brought for bait—well, your little brother is eating it." He looked like he was going to lose his breakfast.

"Tim. Quit eating the bait. Give me that." Rick grabbed the bag from Tim's hands, and looked inside. "Oh, good. He didn't eat it all." Rick looked at Marcus sheepishly. "I, uh, didn't happen to have aged intestines, so I brought what we could find." He jiggled the bag. "This should work just as well."

"What is it? Let me see." Marcus impatiently stared at the bag in Rick's hands.

"Vjnhadaj," Rick mumbled.

"What?" Marcus demanded.

"I said, 'veggie hot dogs,'" Rick repeated loudly. "They were left over from dinner. It was the closest thing to aged intestines that we had."

"Oh, you've got to be kidding," Marcus howled, dancing around in a circle like a crazy duck. "Are we trying to lure a vegetarian fox? Is that a good selling point? That our furs have lower cholesterol?"

Rick did not see the humor in the situation. "Are you going to help me bait this thing, or do I have to do it myself?"

Marcus finally settled down, and bent over with his hands on his knees as he tried to catch his breath. "OK, man. It's OK," he said, stifling a volcano of laughs. "If it works for you vegetarians, it just might fool the foxes. We'll see. Let's put the, um, veggie dog on the trap."

The boys put the lure on the trap, camouflaged it with grass and leaves, and then set and baited the other two traps further down the trail.

"Whew." Rick wiped the back of his hand across his forehead. "Now I guess we just wait."

"Well, I'm going to have to wait at home." Marcus sighed. "I told my mom I wouldn't be gone too long. I have to help my sister clean the house."

"I'm going home, too," Tim whined, wiping veggie dog from the side of his mouth. "I'm thirsty."

"You guys go on ahead," Rick waved them off. "I'm going to go over and look at the planes at the airport for a while."

As the other boys headed back up toward home, Rick hiked down through the trees until he emerged from the woods and onto the moist green grass next to the airport. He walked across the open field to the airplane hangar, and pushed the door open.

"Hello?" Rick peered inside and waited for his eyes to adjust to the darkened room.

"Oh, hi there, Rick," came a voice from the other side of a dismantled engine. "Hand me that wrench over there, would ya?"

Rick walked over to the table, picked up the tool, and put it into the greasy hand of Rob, one of the mechanics. He and Jim, the other mechanic, liked Rick and always let him hang out with them in the hangar.

"I heard Mr. Schwartz fly in this morning," Rick said.

"Oh, yeah. That guy is the craziest pilot in the whole state of Washington. He loves to storm us before he lands," Jim grunted as he and Rob worked. "He scares me half to death with his crazy antics. One of these days he's going to lay that P-51 down on a nose or a wing instead of wheels. I just hope I'm out of the way when it happens."

Rob came out from under the engine and looked at Rick with a half-smile. "Want to help us work on this engine? I'll show you what to do."

Rob and Jim were both pretty cool guys, and they liked having Rick around. They knew that Rick wanted to be a missionary bush pilot, and sometimes they actually seemed impressed with the stuff Rick already knew about airplanes. Rick spent the rest of the morning in the hangar, talking airplanes with Rob and Jim while they worked.

"Here's a bit of advice," Rob said, pointing his wrench at Rick. "If you ever take a plane engine apart, and put it back together, and find that you have extra pieces leftover? Don't fly the plane anywhere."

"You're the expert," Rick said with a bow as Jim rolled his eyes.

When Rick arrived home, Mom was in the kitchen. "I'm getting ready to make lunch," she said. "Why don't you and Tim practice your trumpets until we're ready to eat?"

Rick went into the living room, pulled his shiny trumpet out of its case, and popped his lips together to loosen them up. He didn't mind practicing—he actually liked it—and he and Tim had even played several special trumpet duets at church.

"Come on, Tim," he called. "Let's practice that new duet we've been working on."

They laid out their sheet music across the back of the couch and began playing the melody—first Tim, then Rick, then the two of them together. The smooth sound of the notes filled the house, and even Chris and Laurie stopped playing with their toys and came in to listen.

"Sounds good," Mom called from the kitchen.

When lunch was over, Mom put Chris and Laurie down for a nap. "Whew, those two keep me busy," she said. "The only time I can get anything done is when they're asleep." She laughed as she kissed Tim on the head. "Hey, I'm going to go work on weeding that front flowerbed. Will you guys help me? The more hands we have weeding, the less time it will take."

Rick and Tim grabbed their gardening gloves out of the garage and knelt next to Mom in the grass by the flowers.

"Have you met the new neighbors yet?" she asked as they pulled the pesky weeds out of the black dirt.

"No," Rick said. "I thought I saw a kid my age yesterday, but I wasn't sure."

"They seem really nice," Mom said, pulling her gardening gloves off and pushing her hair out of her eyes. The fingers of the gloves were already crusted with dirt. "I met them this morning. It's a mom and a son who's your age, Rick. His name is Ben. I told him about you. You should stop by and say hello."

"You mean, just go over and introduce myself like the neighborhood welcome parade? I'll look like a dork."

Mom shook her head. "It's not dorky to say hello."

Rick got his chance later, when his new neighbor came outside to shoot hoops. "Hey," Rick called, walking across the street. "Are you Ben?"

The kid glanced over his shoulder for a moment, and then kept dribbling his basketball.

"I'm Rick," Rick said as he pointed across the street. "I live over there. You just moved in?"

"Wow, you must be a genius," Ben said sarcastically. He caught the ball and draped his arm over it, as he stood looking at Rick. "How could you tell? By the great big moving truck?"

Rick's eyebrows drew together, and he was quiet for a moment. A hundred retorts dashed through his mind, but he didn't say any of them. Instead he said, "Yeah, we saw the truck. Where'd you move from?"

Ben turned and shot the ball from his fingertips. It swished through the hoop without touching the rim. "I moved from someplace really cool. And now I live in the boring town of Auburn, in this dumpy house, next to stupid people. Are you happy?"

Ben grabbed his ball and strode back inside his house without another word. Rick could feel a surge of anger climbing his chest. "What a nice guy," he mumbled as he turned to go home. So much for trying to be nice.

It was almost dark that night when the phone rang. It was Marcus, and he was frantic. "Rick. You're not going to believe this, but our traps have been sabotaged."

"What do you mean?"

"I mean, somebody set them off and kicked them off the path. We're going to have to start over."

Rick couldn't believe it. Who would do something like that? When he hung up the phone, he could only think of one person—a new kid on the block. A new kid with a bad attitude.

Chapter 4

"Not again." Rick jerked his baseball cap off of his head and tossed it in the grass as he sat on his bike staring at the traps. Since he and Marcus had first set them up, this was the third time someone had come along and sabotaged them.

"This is ridiculous." Marcus climbed off of his bike, pushed the kickstand into place, and squatted down to survey the damage. "Why does someone keep doing this?"

"I don't know why, but I'm pretty sure I know who," Rick said grimly. "I think it's that new neighbor kid. I told you what he said to me the other day."

"Yeah, he seems like a jerk, but that still doesn't explain his motive." Marcus massaged his temples with his fingers. "Besides, we can't prove it, and we can't go around making accusations on a hunch. What are we going to do?"

"First of all, let's move the traps to a new location." Rick chewed his bottom lip as he thought. "If he doesn't know where they are, he can't sabotage them."

"Good idea," Marcus agreed.

"Second of all," Rick continued, "I'm going to keep my eyes open. I don't care how good he is. One of these days he's going to slip up, and we'll catch him in the act."

Marcus posted lookout duty with his dad's old binoculars to see if they were being followed, and Rick carried the traps deeper into the woods, careful not to leave tracks or any other indication of where the traps were being repositioned.

"There," Marcus sighed when they had reset the last trap. "What now?"

"We'll keep checking. And let's walk the trapline every hour or so, just to be safe," Rick decided.

"I guess we're going to have to get used to this." Marcus looked at Rick seriously. "I mean, right now it's a neighbor kid trying to undermine our objective. When we're missionaries in a foreign country, it could be border patrols and infidels. Maybe this is just practice."

Rick's eyes flashed. "You're right. Maybe we're being tested to see if we can handle the job. Well, I think we're up to it. What should our plan of action be?"

Marcus thought for a moment. "What about that 'fiery coals' thing in the Bible? You know, be nice to your enemy, because that's like heaping coals of fire on his head?"

"Yeah," Rick said slowly. "We could kill him with kindness. It's not going to be easy, though, because, like I said, that kid's a jerk."

"We just have to keep being nice, over and over, no matter how mean he is back to us," Marcus answered. "We'll wear him down. In the meantime, we'll watch our backs."

The boys launched a strategy, and agreed that whenever they saw Ben they'd wave and be friendly and invite him to do stuff with them—such as playing catch or going bike riding. They called their plan Operation Fiery Coals.

Riding their bikes, it only took a few minutes to get from the woods to Ben's front door. They parked out front and rang the doorbell. It was a while before Ben's mom appeared at the door. Her eyes looked puffy and red, like she'd been crying, but she smiled at them. "Hi guys. What can I do for you?"

"Hi," Rick said. "We were just wondering if maybe Ben wants to come out and go bike riding with us."

Ben's mom shook her head. "Sorry, Ben isn't here. He went for a walk." She blinked rapidly, as if she was trying not to cry. "You could try back later," she added.

"Thanks," Marcus said.

Ben's mom closed the front door, and the boys climbed back onto their bikes. "She looked like she was crying," Marcus whispered. "I wonder what's wrong."

"I don't know," Rick said as they wheeled onto the sidewalk and continued down the street. "It's kind of weird. Maybe she didn't want to move here, either."

Marcus skidded to a stop, and Rick almost rode right into him. "What are you doing?" Rick demanded, gripping his handlebars and extending his right leg to steady himself.

"I just thought of something. She said that Ben went for a walk. If you were going to go for a walk, where would you go?" Marcus lifted one eyebrow and looked at Rick.

"Probably to the woods to—" Rick stopped suddenly. "The woods!" he exclaimed. "Our traps!"

"Let's go." Marcus slammed his foot down on his bike pedal and peeled a black mark on the sidewalk as he sped off. Rick wasn't far behind. They followed the sidewalk to the end, and then rode off the ledge and landed their bike tires on the rocky trail.

"Hurry!" Rick shouted. "Let's catch him."

Rick pedaled faster, dodging tree branches and blackberry bushes as he skidded almost out of control on the narrow path. Marcus rode in front of him, catching air on exposed tree roots and mastering the quick turns with a flick of his wrist on the handlebars.

"Do you see him?" Rick said in a hoarse whisper when they stopped at the edge of the animal path, trying to catch their breath.

Marcus shook his head and peered through the trees. "Let's go see," he whispered back.

Rick and Marcus quietly laid their bikes in the bushes and tiptoed down the path. A twig snapped, and both boys dove behind some bushes to keep from being seen.

"I saw movement," Rick said in a low voice, pointing through the bushes. "Someone's over there."

Marcus slowly raised his head and pulled the branches apart, then sat down again with wide eyes. "Not someone," he whispered. "It's something. Caught in one of the traps."

"A fox?" Rick asked excitedly.

Marcus shook his head. "I don't think so," he said slowly. "It's black and white."

Rick and Marcus stood up and looked over the bushes at the trap. "A *skunk*," Rick said, his mouth hanging open. "We got a skunk."

"Oh, this is not good." Marcus shook his head. "Who wants to buy skunk fur?"

"Nobody." Rick sank to the ground and rested his cheek on his fist.

"We could spray paint the white stripe to match the black." Marcus acted as if someone turned a light bulb on in his head. "No one would ever know."

Rick rolled his eyes and absently twirled dry grass between his fingers. "Nice try, Einstein, but don't you think they'd smell the paint?"

"It might cover up the smell of the skunk fur." Marcus kicked a stone into the bushes and plopped down next to Rick. "Besides, it was *your* brilliant idea to use veggie dogs for a lure instead of aged intestines. That's probably why we got a skunk."

"Yeah?" Rick said, setting his jaw. "Well, at least I—" he stopped. "You know, arguing isn't going to get us anywhere. On the other side of these bushes, there's a skunk caught in our trap. What are we going to do now?"

Marcus sighed deeply. "What do mean, what are we going to do? We have to put it out of its misery."

"Kill it?" Rick turned his head sharply to look at Marcus.

"Of course. We can't get close enough to push the release lever. It'd spray us. Or even worse, it might bite us."

"I don't know." Rick seemed to be thinking. "A *little* bite wouldn't be as bad as a big spray."

"You're crazy." Marcus laughed. "Go on now. Do it. Trapping was your idea."

"But I don't want to—*kill it*," Rick said again, standing up to look at the trapped skunk.

Through the branches, Rick could see its little pointed face and fluffy black and white tail. One leg was caught between the metal jaws. The rest of its furry body stretched as far away from the trap as it could go. Rick felt a catch in his throat as he watched the confused animal tug at the trap in terror.

Marcus wrinkled his forehead. "What did you think we were going to do when we caught something? Did you think we'd come out to the trapline one day and find a fur coat, with buttons and everything, sitting in the trap?"

"No," Rick said, "I just didn't really think about what it would be like to actually—" His voice trailed off as he looked at the skunk.

Marcus stood, dusted himself off, and clamped his hand on Rick's shoulder. "It has to be done. It's the only way. Let's go get your bow and arrow set and do what we have to do."

Rick's feet felt like they were made of lead as he and Marcus trudged into the garage and pulled out the bow and the arrows.

"What are you going to do with that?" Tim demanded as he came through the door and saw the bow and arrows in Rick's hands. "Are you going hunting? I want to come. I know how to hunt for wild animals. I'm a good hunter."

"When have you ever been hunting?" Rick shook his head and rolled his eyes at Tim.

"Duh! Where you do think I got the ants in my ant farm? Do you think they just came crawling in? No. I hunted them," Tim said indignantly. "I had to stalk them quietly, and grab them before they saw me."

Marcus snickered. "Ants are not exactly wild animals. They're not even dangerous."

Tim frowned. "Some of them were red ants. Those are dangerous."

"Whatever," Rick said. "The point is, you can't come with us, because we need you to keep watch on the house. It's very important that you protect Mom and Chris and Laurie while we're gone."

"Yeah," Marcus added as he and Rick rolled their bikes out of the garage. "And if you see any wild animals, stalk them, and grab them before they see you."

"OK," Tim called, waving cheerfully as they rode away.

A few minutes later, Rick and Marcus crawled through the bushes and stopped a safe distance away from the skunk. It had stopped struggling, and just stood there, watching them. The woods were quiet except for a buzzing bee that was trying to navigate around a spiderweb. The boys lay in the warm grass in silence.

Finally, Rick handed Marcus the bow. "You do it, man. I don't think I can."

Marcus didn't seem as confident as he had before. He reached for an arrow, pulled it back in the bow, and took aim at the little creature. After a deep breath, he closed his eyes and let the arrow fly.

Ping. The arrow left the bow and whizzed past the bushes toward the skunk.

"You missed it by, like, two feet on the left," Rick reported, looking at the wayward arrow. "Maybe you should try it with your eyes open."

Marcus opened his eyes and picked up another arrow. Aiming further to the right, he let the arrow sail from the bow. This time, it missed the skunk on the right side.

Rick buried his face in his hands and shook his head.

"Hey, I'm nervous, OK?" Marcus said defensively. "Give me another arrow. I'll get it this time."

The third arrow also missed the mark and landed in the dirt in front of the skunk.

"We only have two arrows left," Rick hissed. "Give me that. I'll just do it and get it over with."

Rick's aim was no better, and soon all five arrows lay scattered around the missed target.

"Now what are we going to do?" moaned Marcus.

Rick surveyed the situation. "I have an idea," he said. "Remember what Tim said about stalking the ants real quietly?"

Marcus rolled over on his back and crossed his arms. "Uh-huh, but what does that have to do with *this?*" he nodded his head back toward the skunk.

"Well, let's get Tim, and while you and I distract the skunk by making noise, he could sneak over and get the arrows for us," Rick said reasonably. "He's smaller and will make less commotion."

Tim did not want to be relieved of his post. "I can't go to the woods with you. I'm protecting Mom and Chris and Laurie from wild animals."

"But we found the wild animal in the woods, and now we need your help," Rick implored. "We need someone who knows how to stalk a wild animal without being seen. Tim, we need you to be the, uh, weapons retrieval engineer."

Marcus gave Rick a "thumbs-up" behind Tim's back as they waited for Tim to mull over the idea.

Tim seemed to like the fancy title, and after a moment, he nodded. "OK," he said. "I'll do it."

The skunk hadn't moved. Of course, the trap was a little heavy to drag, but the boys were glad to see that he was just where they'd left him.

"See those arrows scattered by the skunk?" Rick pointed Tim's face in the right direction. Tim nodded. "Marcus and me are going to distract him, and you crawl over and get the arrows when he's not looking your way. Got it?"

Rick helped Tim get down on his belly and instructed him to wait until he and Marcus could hike around to the other side and get the skunk's attention. The plan worked beautifully. Rick and Marcus yelled and beat the bushes with sticks, and Tim sneaked up behind the skunk, picking up arrow after arrow. The last arrow was the closest to the skunk, and he stretched out his little fingers as far as he could to reach it.

"Keep going, Tim," Rick and Marcus shouted, still making noise for the skunk. "You've almost got it."

Rick saw Tim lunge closer to grab the arrow, and at that moment, the skunk realized that something important was going on behind him.

Rick gasped and held his breath as Tim and the startled skunk stared at each other, face to face.

Chapter 5

Rick and Marcus stopped shouting and helplessly watched the showdown between Tim and the skunk.

"Don't move," Rick hissed.

For a moment, both Tim and the skunk were perfectly still, eye to eye.

The skunk stomped its back feet.

Startled, Tim gave a little hop.

Then pandemonium broke loose.

In a flash of black and white, the skunk whipped its hind legs up over its head and sent a steady stream of sour, yellowish liquid straight toward Tim's chest. The skunk, unlike the boys, had perfect aim, and in an instant, the front of Tim's shirt was dripping with a stinky, oily musk that could put an NFL locker room to shame.

"Aaaah!" Tim jumped up, stumbling around and flailing his arms in the air like a windmill. The arrows went flying in all directions. "It shot me with its venom," he gasped. "I can't breathe."

"Neither can I," Marcus wheezed, falling on the

ground and rolling around in the pine needles as he laughed at the sight of Tim.

"Get up." Rick looked at Marcus in disgust, and tried to shield his own nose from the burning stench.

"I can't see," Tim choked and gagged, grabbing at his chest. "I'm blind."

As Tim tripped backwards, his foot landed on the spring release. The trap jaws opened. The skunk, free from the trap and out of spray, scampered quickly into the thick bushes and disappeared.

Rick ventured closer to Tim, and pulled his T-shirt up over his face. "You're not blind—it didn't even get near your eyes," he said. "Stop jumping around. It's not venom—it's just skunk spray, and it's not exactly lethal. You're going to be fine."

"I stink," Tim wailed.

"That's never bothered you before," Rick countered, grabbing Tim by the shoulders. "Get a grip. We have to figure out what to do next. Marcus is right. Mom's going to freak out like never before in history."

His hands clapped over his nose, Marcus walked all around Tim. "Hmm, we could spray him off with the garden hose," he suggested. "Or he could take his clothes off—they're what's really stinky—and wash them in the river."

"No!" Tim said fiercely. "I'm not being naked."

"Those are good ideas," Rick said. "But I don't think they're going to work. The first one will make Mom suspicious, and the second one, well, that's not even something I want to picture in my head."

"We'll just have to air him out then," Marcus said. "If we keep him outside all afternoon, maybe the smell will go away."

"I want to go home," Tim said with a trembling lower lip as he looked down at his soiled shirt.

"Do you really want to go back home and be stuck playing with Chris and Laurie and their baby toys," Rick said carefully. "Or, do you want to hang out with me and Marcus and explore?"

Rick's proposition turned out to be irresistible, and the boys spent all afternoon climbing the tall, swaying trees and swinging from branch to branch. When they knew they couldn't stay away any longer, they began shuffling toward home.

"Well, what do you think?" Tim asked, looking up at Rick and Marcus. "Do I smell better?"

"I actually don't smell anything anymore," Marcus said. "I think we aired you out enough. I'm sure your mom will never know."

"I don't smell anything either," Rick said. "But it might be because my smeller is burnt to a crisp from the initial blast."

"I think I smell fine," Tim said. "Besides, I'm hungry, and I want dinner."

"Well, good luck. Catch you later." Marcus gave Rick and Tim a snappy salute before he jumped over the fence and headed home.

"Well, here goes," Rick breathed to himself as

they walked in through the sliding glass door. "Hi, Mom," he called. "Is dinner almost ready?"

Mom came around the corner with a scrunched nose and frowning lips. "What in the world is that smell?" she demanded.

Rick took a deep breath. "Smells like lentil stew—my favorite," he said, noticing the pot on the stove. "Smells great, Mom."

But Mom had put her hand over her nose and was backing away from the boys. "I don't—" she started to say, but Tim cut in.

"I smell like a skunk because a skunk sprayed me because Rick and Marcus set up their traps and a skunk got in it and they shot at it with arrows and lost them and they made me go get them and the skunk sprayed me on my shirt and that's why I stink," Tim said in one breath before Rick could clamp a hand over his mouth.

Mom crossed her arms and spoke in a low, carefully measured voice. "Go outside," she said to Tim. "Take off every bit of clothing that is on your body. I'll throw out a towel for you to cover with. Then come into the house and get into the bathtub. Luckily, I stocked up on tomato juice the last time I went to the bulk food store, because you're going to bathe in it."

"And you," Mom said, turning a sharp eye on Rick, "go to the garage and get a shovel. You are going to take your little brother's clothing into the woods. You're going to dig a deep hole. You are going to put the clothes in the hole. You are going to cover them up with a lot of dirt. And when you are finished, we will discuss the events that led up to today's skunk incident." She sounded like a drill sergeant. "Do you understand me?"

Rick blinked and nodded. He understood.

When Rick finished burying the clothes, he went back inside the house to find Mom in the bathroom with several very large empty tomato juice cans, overseeing Tim's bathing and skunk odor removal operations.

Just then Dad stepped through the doorway behind him, still wearing his hospital scrubs. "What's this?" he asked in surprise. It wasn't every day that he saw one of his sons sitting in a bathtub full of tomato juice. "I hope this isn't what we're having for dinner."

Dad laughed at his own joke, but no one else was in a humorous mood—especially Rick. Not only had his trap investment gone south, but it had gotten him into trouble in the process. And after everything they'd been through, he was not a penny closer to that Super Cub.

Chapter 6

The bad news: Rick was grounded for a week from anything that might be considered fun and saddled with enough chores to exhaust a pack mule. Not only that, but his mom made him return the metal traps to Mr. Bushnell.

The good news: Mr. Bushnell was nice enough to give back the money they'd paid him, Mom had let him get a paper route, and while Rick was at home doing yard chores, he could still spy on Ben. Thus, Operation Fiery Coals was still in full effect. Sometimes Rick wondered if Ben was watching him out of the corner of his eye, but every time Rick waved and said hello, Ben scowled and turned away.

One day, Ben's mom came out and talked to him while he was making shots at the basketball hoop. When she tried to give him a hug, Ben pushed her away, went into the house and slammed the door. Ben's mom sat on the front porch for a long time before she went inside.

"What is wrong with that guy?" Marcus asked when Rick reported his findings about Ben over the phone the next day. "He's not even nice to his own mother."

"I don't know." Rick was cradling the phone between his ear and his shoulder while he thumbed through his flight magazine. "He's weird, that's for sure. Hey, guess what? I got a paper route."

"You did?" Marcus sounded surprised. "I thought you were grounded."

"Not anymore," Rick said. "Mom said I needed a better-smelling source of income, so she helped me get a paper route. Tim wants to help me with it. And I'm going to get a savings account at the bank, too, so we can save up money for our plane."

"That's awesome," Marcus said. "Hey, now that you're not stuck at home anymore, do you want to go down to the river? We could pan for gold."

Rick snorted. "Last time we did that, we found two nails and a girl's hair clip."

"You give up too easily," Marcus chided. "Maybe we just haven't looked in the right place yet. Besides, if we found a nice vein of gold in the river, you could own the newspaper and hire someone else to deliver it."

"All right," Rick said. "I guess I could use a swim anyway. But what are we going to do with Tim? He's going to want to follow us."

"Oh, man," Marcus moaned. "I'm glad my parents have spared me the pain and agony of a younger brother. I'm so lucky."

"Marcus, you *are* the younger brother, remember? Your sister is the one with a little brother, and I think your luck comes from *being* the pain and agony," Rick retorted. "Besides, Tim's not that bad. We just have to find a way to keep him busy. He'll want to be involved in anything we do to try to earn money."

"Just for the record, my sister is weird and deserves every bit of pain and agony I give her. But I see your point. We should find a way to help Tim earn his own money," Marcus suggested. "Maybe he could sing door-to-door, or take pledges and stand on his head for a couple of days to raise money, I don't know."

"What about a fruit punch stand?" Rick said, the idea dawning on him. "We could set him up with a little table and a pitcher of fruit punch, and he could sell paper cups full for, like, 25 cents apiece."

"That would keep him busy," Marcus agreed. "I like it."

Tim liked the idea, too, and willingly took up residence on the front lawn with a table and a sign. He promised to donate all of his fruit punch proceeds to the airplane fund, and seemed to be content as he watched for cars with potential customers to come down the street.

"There you go, buddy. Make lots of money," Rick encouraged Tim as he pulled his bicycle out of the garage and followed Marcus down the street. "And keep the ants out of the punch. It could be bad for sales." Tim gave Rick and Marcus a thumbs up sign as they rode away on their bicycles toward the river.

The sun was hot, and the clouds were sparse in the blue sky. The boys could hardly wait to cool off. Light danced on the water in ripples of sparkles in the shallow river. Rick and Marcus laid their bikes down at the forest edge and tiptoed barefoot over the hot river rock until they sank their toes into the refreshing water that slapped at their ankles and darkened their pant legs.

Suddenly, Marcus stood still. "Did you see something over there?" he said, pointing toward the woods.

"Nice try," Rick said. "You want me to turn my head so you can douse me with water?"

"No, I'm serious. Over there, by the woods," Marcus said, pointing. "I think I saw movement by the tree. Someone was just messing with our bikes."

Rick didn't see anything, but they both waded out of the water and splashed their way over the river rock toward where their bikes lay.

As they came closer, Marcus' suspicions were confirmed. Someone had slashed their bicycle tires. Rick and Marcus stared, shocked, at the gaping holes in the deflated tires.

"Who—?" Rick exclaimed, trying to peer in through the trees.

Marcus looked determined. "Let's go get him."

Rick and Marcus took off into the woods, running barefoot down the path and weaving in around the trees as they looked for the culprit. When they finally gave up their search, they returned to their bicycles, out of breath and discouraged.

"I've had it," Rick sputtered.

"Me, too," Marcus agreed, kicking his bike tire with his heel. "We've got to catch this guy."

Rick and Marcus slipped their sockless feet into their tennis shoes, and started walking their bikes back up the trail. By the time they reached Rick's front yard, they were sweaty, and tired, and irritable from the whole situation.

Tim was still sitting at his little table, swinging his bare feet back and forth in the grass under his chair. "Hi guys," he called.

"I'm not in the mood to talk," Rick said in a grumpy tone. "Somebody slashed our bike tires, and we had to walk all the way home."

"Yeah, and I'm getting tired of this," Marcus said. "I'm about ready to just— Hey, what's that on Tim's lip?"

"What's what?" Rick looked at Tim closely, then realized what Marcus was talking about. "Tim," Rick said sternly. "Why do you have a fruit punch mustache?"

"It's hot outside," Tim said. "I was thirsty."

Rick and Marcus looked into the fruit punch pitcher and shook their heads at each other. "Tim, this pitcher is empty," Rick stated the obvious. "How much of it did you sell?"

Tim paused. "None, but—"

"You drank it all?" Rick exploded.

"Yes, but—"

"You are unbelievable," Rick shouted. "Can't you do anything right?"

Tim's shoulders drooped, and his lower lip quivered. "I'm sorry, but—" Tim started to cry big tears that rolled down his cheeks and splashed onto his T-shirt. "I didn't mean to drink it all, I just—"

"Great!" Marcus said, pushing Rick in the arm. "Now you made him cry."

Rick looked down at his little brother and felt sorry. He knelt down and put a hand on Tim's shoulder. "No, it's OK. I'm sorry for yelling. I'm just really frustrated because our bike tires got slashed, and then we got back, and you didn't make any money with the fruit punch stand, and—"

"But I did make money," Tim said, wiping his nose with the back of his hand. "I made $10. See?" He pulled a crumpled $10 bill out of his pocket and handed it to Rick.

"Where did you get this?" Rick asked, turning it over in his hand.

"From that lady who lives down the street. She stopped her car and said she wasn't thirsty, but she gave me $10 'cause I'm cute." Tim grinned a little under his fruit punch mustache.

"Oh, man," Marcus said to Rick. "We work and work and don't make a dime, and your little brother just sits there and makes 10 bucks. This is great."

"I guess it's a good thing I'm your partner, huh?" Tim said triumphantly.

Rick smiled down at him. "Yes, it's a good thing. And, when it comes time to collect the money from the customers on our paper route, I'm sending you to do the talking."

"Why?" Tim asked.

"Because," Rick teased, pinching Tim's cheeks, "you're soooo cute."

Chapter 7

Rick yawned and rolled over as he stuffed his face into his pillow and pulled his covers tight in around his neck. He took a deep breath and had just started to drift back into dreamland when he felt a strange sensation of warm air on his cheek.

"Time to get up!" Tim yelled directly into Rick's ear, and Rick jumped up in a rush of adrenaline that snapped his eyelids open and almost made him bump his head on the underside of the top bunk. Rick sat there blindly for an instant until he realized what had happened.

Tim giggled and tried to duck out of reach as Rick shoved the covers aside to tackle him. "Haven't you ever heard of an *indoor* voice?" Rick said through gritted teeth as he rubbed his knuckles on Tim's head.

"I *did* use my indoor voice," Tim said, his giggling voice muffled by the carpet. "Twice—but you didn't wake up. Dad says if we don't get up and get going now, he won't have time to take us on our paper route before work. And then we'll have to walk, because your bicycle tires are still slashed."

Rick let go, and Tim sat up, his hair pointing every which way from the knuckle rub, as Rick nodded thoughtfully. "Good point. OK, I guess I will let you off the hook this time since you have a good reason. But don't ever wake me up like that again. You scared the pajamas off of me."

Dad and Tim were in the kitchen rolling the Auburn *Globe* newspapers and wrapping rubber bands around them when Rick came stumbling down the stairs.

"Are you hungry?" Dad asked. "I just popped in a couple more pieces of toast."

Rick shook his head as he grabbed a rubber band and started rolling a newspaper. "No thanks. I don't think my stomach is open for business yet. It might rebel."

"We don't want that to happen," Dad said, scooping up the last of his rolled newspapers and helping Tim slide them into a bag. "Listen, I'm going to try to get done at the hospital early so I can take your bike downtown and see about getting those tires fixed. Did you say you saw who did it?"

"Not really," Rick said. "All we saw was movement, but by the time we got there, the one who did it was gone." He wanted to tell his dad that he and Marcus suspected Ben, but he knew better than to say anything like that without proof. He shoved his newspaper into the bag and followed Dad and Tim out the door. "We're keeping our eyes open, though.

Whoever's doing it will mess up, and we'll figure it out sooner or later."

Rick and Tim took turns tossing the papers on customers' doorsteps until every house on their route had gotten a morning paper. Rick passed Ben's house on the way home, and looked around, hoping to find clues. Unfortunately, he found nothing, and the house was quiet.

Mom was still in her bathrobe in the kitchen with Laurie and Chris when Dad dropped Tim and Rick off back at home. Chris and Laurie were making a mess of their oatmeal, and Mom was eating an orange wedge. "Hi, guys. How was your first day on the job?"

"Good," Rick said, sitting down at a chair at the table and letting the newspaper bag slide off of his shoulder. "I'm glad Dad drove us today. It would have been a long walk."

"Are those extra?" Mom asked, looking at the newspapers that were still in the bag.

"Yeah," Rick said. "They always give us extra for emergencies, but we can have them if we don't use them for customers. Do you want to read one?"

"Sure, thanks," Mom said, wiping her hands on a paper towel. She unrolled one of the papers and opened it up on the counter, reading while she spooned some oatmeal into bowls for Rick and Tim.

"Good job today, partner," Rick said to Tim as Mom put steaming bowls in front of them. "We make a good team. And, with every paycheck we put into our savings account, we're that much closer to buying our Super Cub airplane."

"How much do you have so far?" Mom asked, still browsing through the paper.

Rick blew on his spoon to cool the oatmeal. "Well, as of last week when we all deposited our allowance, we had $206.76."

"Plus the $10 I made with the fruit-juice stand," Tim interjected.

"Yeah," Rick said. "So that brings us to $216.76."

Mom looked up from the newspaper, obviously impressed. "Not bad," she said. "You guys are pretty dedicated."

"Yeah, well, we still have a long way to go," Rick answered after swallowing.

"Hey, look at this," Mom said, picking up the paper and reading aloud. "'Community Center Talent Show, all ages. First prize in all categories, $50.' It happens in one month."

"Fifty dollars?" Tim's eyes widened as he looked at Rick. "That's a lot of money."

Mom thought for a moment. "Why don't we enter you into the talent show? You two could play that great trumpet piece that you've been working on."

"Do you think we could win?" Rick asked doubtfully.

"Do I think you could win?" Mom repeated with a laugh. "I think you have an excellent chance of winning. Whenever the two of you play that trumpet duet, it's so beautiful I could cry. I know other people would love it, too."

"Let's do it," Tim said, sliding off of his chair to take his bowl to the sink.

Rick nodded. "I agree. We should do it. Mom, will you enter us into the show?"

"Of course," Mom said. "You have a whole month to practice your trumpets and perfect the piece. I think it will be a showstopper."

Rick and Tim spent most of the day inside, practicing their trumpets until their lips were numb.

"It sounds awesome, guys," Mom said, clapping.

"My lips are going to fall off of my face, and I'm going to look like a freak if we don't take a break," Tim said finally. ·

"All right, all right. We deserve a break." Rick put his trumpet back in the case and gathered their music into a stack. "We'll practice more tomorrow."

As promised, Dad was home early, and Marcus and Rick helped him load Rick's bike into the trunk of the car to take it to downtown Auburn to the bike shop. Mom and Chris and Laurie decided to go along.

"You and Tim can stay here if you want," Mom offered to Rick. "We won't be gone that long, and if there's any kind of emergency, Marcus's sister is home."

"My sister *is* an emergency," Marcus muttered to Rick.

Rick punched Marcus in the ribs. "We'll be fine, Mom. And I'll keep an eye on Tim."

"OK, see you in a few," Mom said, rolling up her window as Dad started the car. "Tim, listen to Rick!"

"Oh, one more thing," Dad said. "Don't ride your mom's bike. I need to work on it. I'll have your bike back soon with new tires."

Rick waved as his parents pulled out of the driveway and down the street.

"So, what do you want to do?" Marcus asked. "Terrorize my sister? Raid the refrigerator? Go skunk hunting?"

Rick made a face. "Very funny."

As the boys stood in the yard deciding what to do, the garage door on Ben's house slowly creaked open, and Ben came out.

"Hey, Ben," Rick called and waved, staying true to their Operation Fiery Coals strategy.

"Want to come over and play a game or something with us?" Marcus asked, looking across the street to where Ben stood.

"Like what?" Ben smirked. "Are you girls going to draw chalk squares on the sidewalk and play hopscotch?"

"I'm not a girl," Tim announced.

"Shhh. He knows that," Rick said softly to Tim. "He was just trying to insult us. Don't let it bother you."

"I've only played hopscotch twice," Marcus said defensively. "And my sister Carlie made me."

"Whatever. I've got better things to do, so why don't you weirdos go be stupid somewhere else." Ben pulled some tools out of a toolbox and bent over to work on his skateboard.

Rick and Marcus shook their heads in disbelief as they looked at each other, then back at Ben.

"Forget it," Tim said. "Let's play tag. I'm it."

Immediately, Tim poked Rick in the ribs, and ran off giggling. "Now you're it," he shouted.

Rick took off after him, but Tim moved like lightning around the yard, darting behind trees and zigzagging between bushes, and Rick couldn't quite catch him.

"Get him, Rick," Marcus yelled, careful to keep himself out of Rick's way so he wouldn't be "it" next.

Rick finally stopped, panting as he shook his head at Tim. "You've gotten faster, little man," he wheezed in surprise.

"Oh, now that's pathetic," Ben called from across the street. "Your little brother can outrun you? He's like, half your size. You're such a doorknob."

Rick's face started to feel warm as he heard Ben's taunting voice.

"Ignore him," Marcus said in a low voice. "Let's just play the game."

Ben kept talking. "Do you ride to school on the little bus, Rick?" he jeered. "With the rest of the *special* people?"

Rick could feel the hair on the back of his neck stand on end as Ben's mean words hit their mark. He stood still for a moment, fists clenched, adrenaline pumping through his veins as he decided what to do next.

"I'm over here," Tim yelled, waiting on the other side of the yard for Rick to pursue him again. "Nah nah, nah nah, nah naaaaah."

At the sight of Ben's sneering face, Rick paused, then ran into the garage and grabbed his mom's bike down off of the rack. "I'm coming, Tim," he yelled, slamming his foot down on the pedal and wheeling across the yard toward his younger brother. "Watch out now!"

Laughing and screaming, Tim ran behind the bushes, past the side of the house and around to the backyard with Rick tailing close behind. "I've almost got you!" Rick shouted, gripping the handlebars with both hands.

They curved around the yard, and Tim changed direction, running for the sliding glass door. "Can't catch me in here," he teased, running inside the house and throwing the sliding glass door shut behind him.

Rick neared the back porch, squeezing the hand brakes to stop the bike. Nothing happened. Absolutely nothing, except that the bike kept rolling. Horrified, he pumped the brakes again. Again! The bike had picked up speed and now careened toward the glass door. In a split second he remembered why his dad had told him not to ride Mom's bike.

"The brakes don't work!" Rick yelled as he jerked the handlebars, trying to avoid the inevitable.

Time stood still as the bike slammed into the edge of the patio. The momentum of the sudden jolt threw Rick toward the door. He had no time to think. There was nothing he could do to stop it. He crashed through the door and slid headfirst across the kitchen floor in a shower of broken glass.

Chapter 8

Rick lay there in shock, trying to catch his breath. Shards of glass fell around him. The edges of some were stuck into the linoleum right next to his face.

There was no sound except the crunch of Tim's feet on the glass. Tim stood above Rick, his mouth hanging open. "Rick, are you *dead?*" Tim asked, starting to cry.

"I don't think so," Rick answered. He hardly dared move for fear of being cut, but he edged himself up on one knee then held out his hand to his little brother. Tim grasped it and braced himself. Rick pulled himself to his feet just as Marcus pounded up to the doorway.

Ignoring him, Rick slowly searched himself for cuts. Somehow he seemed to be watching himself from a distance. Shards of glass fell from his clothes with a tinkling sound as they hit the glass-covered floor.

Marcus shuddered as he looked at the jagged pieces of glass sticking up like weeds from the floor. "Man, Rick, those could've stuck in *you.*"

A moment later, Ben sauntered up, too. Rick

thought he looked concerned, but when he saw that Rick was OK, he shrugged. "Wow! I guess you're busted when your parents get home—but I'm sure your daddy will help you clean it up. Have fun." Ben turned and walked back home, leaving the three boys wordlessly staring at each other and at the mess of glass.

Finally Rick spoke. "We've got to clean this up. Ben was right about one thing—I'm busted."

Suddenly Marcus took control. "Tim and I will sweep this up," he said. "You go put on some bandages. You're bleeding." Marcus reached for the broom as Rick headed upstairs to the bathroom.

To his surprise, Rick found only a few nicks and cuts though he had a slight headache. By the time he got downstairs, all the glass had been swept up and Tim had rolled Mom's bike back into the garage. He knew his parents would come in through the front door, so they wouldn't notice it right away. He closed the curtain where the sliding glass door had been, hoping he could find a way to tell them before they saw it for themselves. Marcus headed home, and just as Rick was helping Tim close the door on the garage, Mom and Dad pulled into the driveway.

"Tim, let *me* tell them about the door, OK?" Rick said quickly.

"What if they make me tell them?"

"Well, then you can tell them. But they're not going to make you tell them, because I'm going to tell them. So don't tell them."

"OK." Tim rolled his eyes.

"Got it fixed!" Dad said triumphantly as he lifted Rick's bike from the trunk. "Here you go. Now that you have transportation again, the paper route is your responsibility."

"Thanks, Dad," Rick said, wondering if guilt was visibly seeping through his pores. "I, uh—don't—"

"Say no more. You're welcome," Dad said. "Let's go inside and have dinner. Your mom's making veggie pizza."

Rick helped his dad set the table while Mom took the pizza out of the oven and put it on the cooling rack. Tim buckled Laurie into her high chair, and they all sat down to eat.

After the blessing Rick mustered up his courage. "Dad, I have something to tell you," he said

"Oh, yes—tell him," Mom said, cutting Chris's pizza into bite-size pieces. "I'm so excited."

"What?" Rick looked at his mom in surprise.

"Go on. Tell him. The talent show," she prompted him with a nod.

"Oh, that," Rick said miserably.

"What talent show?" Dad asked. He motioned with a large slice of pizza covered with mushrooms, onion, and green peppers. "You're going to be in a talent show?" He bit off a chunk as he looked at Rick.

"Tim and me, I mean, Tim and I are going to play our trumpets in a talent show," Rick said miserably. "First prize is $50." He stared at the broccoli and sweet peppers on his pizza as if he didn't know what it was on his plate.

"You don't sound very excited," Dad said. He took a long swallow of juice, then picked up another slice. "Your mom is a champion pizza maker!" he said with a smile.

"I *am* excited. It's just that, well, we, um, the—" Rick stared at the curtain covering the entryway and tried to think of a way to tell his parents about the broken sliding glass door. But his mind was blank. Not a word came to him that made any sense.

"They practiced a lot today, Bud," Mom told Dad. "It sounds great. I won't be surprised if they win the whole thing."

"Well, good," Dad said. "Those trumpet lessons were worth every penny—" He paused, looking puzzled. "Do you feel a breeze in here?"

Mom nodded. "That sliding glass door must be open. Could you close it, please? It's chilly in here."

Rick held his breath as Dad reached around the curtain for the door handle. When he didn't find it, he pulled the curtain back and stared at the empty door frame. "Melba, there's no glass here."

"There's no—what?" Mom looked at the empty doorway and gasped. "What in the world?" she asked, looking at Rick and Tim.

"Rick and me and Marcus were playing tag and Rick couldn't catch me and that neighbor kid Ben made fun of him so Rick rode Mom's bike to be faster but I went inside and Rick didn't have any brakes and crashed through the door and broke the glass and we cleaned it up but now there's no door," Tim said breathlessly.

"Tim!" Rick exclaimed with wide eyes.

"Rick!" Dad and Mom both said at once.

"I had to tell them what happened," Tim said to Rick defensively. "They made me. With their eyes!"

Rick covered his face with his hand and shook his head.

"You crashed through the glass?" Mom's eyes darted back and forth between Rick and the missing door. "And didn't get hurt?"

"Just a few nicks, Mom. I'm OK." Rick studied his pizza again.

"Rick slid on the floor with his face, and lots of glass rained on him, and some really big sharp pieces stuck in the floor by his head. They almost got into his brain," Tim offered helpfully.

"OK, I don't need to hear any more details." Mom took a deep breath and put her hand over her heart. "I'm glad you're OK. It's a miracle you weren't seriously hurt, but look at my sliding glass door."

"I think we owe a special prayer of thanks for your guardian angels," Dad said, his eyes on the empty doorway. He sighed. "We'll deal with consequences later, guys."

After dinner, Rick and Tim helped their dad put black plastic over the doorway. Dad made some phone calls, and when he finished he came upstairs to where Rick and Tim were sitting in their room.

"Well, I found someone who'll replace the glass at a reduced cost if I remove the door myself and rein-stall it," Dad said, looking down at the paper he'd scribbled notes on while he was on the phone. "It looks like it's only going to be about $100 to fix it."

Rick knew what was coming. "I guess I owe you about 100 bucks then, huh?"

Dad nodded. "I feel badly, Rick. I know you've been saving up money for an airplane. But a respon-sible person pays for his mistakes. And I know you want to be a responsible person."

Rick looked down at the carpet. "I know, Dad. I'll take the money out of our account in the morning."

"I'm not going to add on any more consequences for disobedience. I think crashing through a sliding glass door and spending your money to fix it has prob-ably made a big enough impression," Dad told him.

Rick's head moved slowly up and down. His eyes stung with disappointed tears as he thought about how long it would take to earn another $100, but he rubbed them away furiously and hoped Dad hadn't noticed. "Thanks," he said in a rough voice.

If Dad noticed Rick had been crying, he didn't say anything about it. He just turned to walk back down the stairs.

Tim sat quietly for a moment, and then spoke up. "I shouldn't have teased you to make you catch me," he said. "It was my fault, too."

Rick patted Tim's head. "Nah, don't worry about it. I shouldn't have let Ben get to me. Come on, let's get our pajamas on and get ready for worship. It's been a long day."

Rick and Tim sat quietly through worship. During prayer, they each thanked God that Rick hadn't been seriously hurt in the crash. Tim prayed last, and added, "Lord, please send us another way to earn money for the airplane so that we can be missionaries in the jungle. In Jesus' name, Amen."

They went upstairs, and before plopping down on top of the covers, Rick opened their bedroom window to let in the cool evening air. The last colors of sunset faded into blackness. Soon Tim was sound asleep. But not Rick. He lay in bed staring out the window up at the stars, wishing he could go back in time and change what he'd done. Of course, that was impossible. To make matters worse, Rick noticed some tiny flashing lights in the distance—an airplane making its way across the sky. He turned toward the wall, punched his pillow with his fist until it was fluffy under his head, and took a deep breath, glad that the day was finally over.

Rick felt like he had barely closed his eyes when something jolted him awake. A strange sound was coming in through his window from outside. He lay in bed quietly for a moment listening, and then, silently slid out of bed and tiptoed to the window to look. He didn't see anything in the darkness, but he thought he could hear a shuffling, squeaking sound coming from the front porch.

Rick started to knock on his parents' bedroom door, but changed his mind. What if it was nothing? He'd already caused enough of an uproar for one day. Heart pounding, Rick picked up his baseball bat and inched his way down the stairs toward the front door. Positioning the bat on his shoulder, Rick slowly reached for the doorknob. Regardless of what was on the other side of the door, he was ready.

At least, he *thought* he was.

Chapter 9

Rick held his breath as he reached for the door-knob, slowly turned it, and yanked the door open with all of his strength. Nothing. No one.

He stepped onto the porch and stared out into the night, looking down the street to the right, then to the left. There was nothing to see but the steady glow of streetlights. Standing still, he watched the bushes and carefully scanned the yard for signs of an intruder. Nothing. Rick sighed.

He waited a moment longer, looking into the darkness, then stepped back to go inside and close the door. In that instant Rick realized that the strange noise came from a box on the porch near his feet. Flipping on the porch light, he looked down and saw six squeaking, wriggling puppies.

"Mom! Dad!" Rick whispered loudly as he knocked on their bedroom door. "Come see what someone left on our porch."

Mom and Dad soon came out of their room, wrapping their bathrobes around themselves and yawning.

"Puppies?" Mom asked, looking over Rick's shoulder into the box. "Oh, look at them. How precious. Who would leave these sweet little balls of fuzz on our porch in the middle of the night?" She picked up one of the squirming fluffballs and held it to her face.

Dad shook his head. "Oh, no! *No, no, no.* We don't need any puppies."

"Puppies?" Tim walked down the stairs in his pajamas, rubbing his eyes. "What puppies?"

"Someone left puppies on our porch in the middle of the night. Look at them," Rick said, pulling Tim close so that he could see.

"No, no, no, no!" Dad repeated over and over in a daze, but no one else seemed to be listening. "We're not keeping the puppies. First thing in the morning I'm taking them to the Humane Society, and—"

Dad's words were cut short by Tim's excitement. "It's my answer," he said, pointing to the puppies. "I prayed for God to send us a way to make money, and He sent us puppies."

Rick looked up at his dad. "That's true, Dad. We could raise and feed them and take care of them until they're old enough, and then we could sell them."

The look on Dad's face still said no, and Rick knew he had to do something drastic. He grabbed Tim's face and pointed it toward his dad. "Say 'please,'" Rick whispered.

Tim conjured a puppy-dog face of his own as he looked up at Dad. "Please, Dad?" he asked, his big brown eyes pleading.

Dad took a deep breath, and Rick knew that he was softening. "All right," Dad said finally. "But you have to take care of them. Not your mom. Not me. You feed them, you clean up after them, and as soon as they're old enough, you find homes for them."

"Thanks, Dad." Tim threw his arms around his dad's waist, and Rick grinned as he looked down at the fuzzy little faces in the box.

"Shhh, you'll wake up your little brother and sister," Dad admonished, but it was obvious he couldn't help smiling at Tim's enthusiasm.

"We need to warm them up," Mom said. "We have no idea how long they've been outside."

Mom got one of Laurie's old bottles from a box in the garage and helped Tim and Rick warm up some milk to feed the hungry little puppies. Before long, all of them were fast asleep, piled on top of each other, with round bellies full of warm milk. Mom tucked some rag towels into the box and helped Rick carry them up to his room.

Rick could hardly sleep. He woke up several times to check on the puppies before he finally had to drag himself and Tim out of bed for their paper route. Mom puppy-sat for them until they got back.

"So, how does it feel to be 'dad' to a litter of puppies?" Mom asked, smiling at Rick's droopy eyelids.

"I'm so tired," Rick yawned.

"Reminds me of when you were born," Mom smiled. "But you are worth every sleepless night."

Rick called Marcus to tell him about the bad news about the cost of the sliding glass door repair, and the good news about the puppies. Marcus came over and helped Rick feed the puppies, and then they rode their bikes to the bank together to withdraw the money for the sliding glass door.

"I guess I should have said something when you got your mom's bike out," Marcus told Rick as he opened another glass door and they stepped into the air-conditioned bank lobby.

"I'm the one who did it," Rick said. "It's not like you could have stopped me."

"Yeah, but I could have at least said something. Now we're going to have to work extra hard to make up for the money we've lost." Marcus followed Rick to the teller station and waited while Rick requested the withdrawal.

After she'd counted the money into Rick's hand, the teller smiled. "Is there anything else I can do you for you?"

Rick swallowed. "Could you give us a remaining balance, please?"

"Of course," the teller answered, typing on her keyboard.

"Why bother?" Marcus said quietly. "We have $100 less than we had before. So that leaves us, like, $116."

"OK, here is your balance," the teller said, reading from a screen. "It looks like there's $4,394.14."

"What?" the boys said together.

"Four thousand, three hundred ninety-four dollars and fourteen cents," the teller repeated.

Rick could hardly breathe. Marcus looked like he was going to pass out.

"Are you sure?" Rick asked.

The teller nodded. "That's what it says here. I can give you a printout, if you want."

"So," Rick said carefully, "if I wanted to, how much of that could I take out right now?"

"All of it, I suppose," the teller answered, looking a little concerned. "But that's quite a bit of money to keep in your back pocket." She paused. "Would you like to make an additional withdrawal?"

"No thanks, this will be fine for now," Rick said, grabbing the edge of Marcus' T-shirt and dragging him out the front door.

"Did you hear that?" Rick sputtered.

"The only thing I heard," Marcus said in a daze, "was '$4,394—'"

"And 14 cents," Rick added. "Something's really wrong here."

"All I can say is, this bank has earned *my* business." Marcus saluted the sign above them. "I am officially a loyal customer."

"What are you talking about?" Rick exclaimed. "We can't keep the money. It's not ours."

"Let's not be so hasty," Marcus said. "It's for a good cause, right? Maybe—just maybe—we're *sup-*

posed to have the money to use toward the airplane."

Rick knew that Marcus was wrong, but he kept quiet and followed as Marcus pedaled back down the street. But they hadn't even ridden an entire block before Rick stopped pedaling and wheeled his bike slowly to a stop. "Marcus," he called.

"What are you doing?" Marcus asked over his shoulder, dragging his foot on the ground to slow himself down. He turned the handlebars and coasted over to Rick.

"We've got to go back to the bank," Rick said. "That money isn't ours."

Marcus stared at the sidewalk for a few moments. "I guess you're right. I was starting to feel guilty before you even said anything."

They parked their bikes in front of the bank and went back through the doors to the same teller they'd talked to before.

"Are you back to make another withdrawal?" she asked, looking surprised.

"No," Rick said slowly. "We're back to tell you that most of the money in our account—well, it isn't ours. We don't know how it got there, but we should only have $116.65 left."

"Is there a problem?" A tall man with a manager's name tag came to the window.

"These boys say that there's more money in their account than there should be," the teller said.

The man's brow crinkled as he stared at the

screen. "I'll look into this," he said, scratching his head. He looked at the boys. "Thank you for bringing this to our attention. I know we would have found it eventually, but we certainly appreciate your honesty."

Rick shrugged, a little embarrassed. "It's OK."

"We wouldn't actually have kept it," Marcus told him, still imagining that they truly had that much in the account.

"Well, thank you again."

The bank manager called that afternoon and talked to Mom. She told his story to Dad and Rick while they ate dinner. "Someone hit a wrong number and accidentally deposited funds into Rick's account. The boys told the teller that their account balance was inaccurate."

Her eyes shone as she said it. Rick could feel how proud she was of him.

Dad was too. "I know adults who don't have the integrity that you have," he told him. "I'm proud of you, son."

Rick wouldn't have traded the look of pride on his dad's face for any amount of money.

Chapter 10

Look how fat they're getting." Marcus held up one of the puppies and grinned at its pudgy little body before he gently placed it back into the box. "That puppy formula must be real good for them." The puppy staggered a few steps, then plopped down and started chewing on its brother's ear.

"Hey, stop," Tim reprimanded. "It's not nice to bite."

"It's OK," Rick said to Tim. "They're just playing."

Rick watched the puppies as they rolled around on top of each other for a little while, then tired, snuggled in together for a nap. He knew he was starting to get attached to them, especially a little white one that he'd secretly named Little Lamb.

Just then Mom peeked her head around the corner of the boys' room. "I'm going out to do some shopping and run some errands," she told them. "Carlie is going to come over and babysit Chris and Laurie while I'm gone. She's such a sweet girl, Marcus. She was in the middle of a project with her sewing machine, but she agreed to come over anyway."

"Great!" Marcus said sarcastically. "If my sister is

coming over, then I'm getting out of here. Want to go to the woods or something?"

Rick nodded as he looked at the sleeping puppies. "Sure. Hey, maybe your sister will watch the puppies for us."

"If you go anywhere, take Tim with you, and keep an eye on him," Mom told them.

The windows began to rattle as the sound of an airplane engine grew louder. Mom covered her ears and rolled her eyes as the rattling grew more and more intense, but Rick and Marcus looked at each other in excitement.

"It's Mr. Schwartz," Rick said excitedly. "He must be doing his regular low flyover before he lands at the airport. Let's go look at the P-51 Mustang."

The boys ran to the window just in time to see the underbelly of Mr. Schwartz's plane fly overhead.

"That was way too close for comfort," Mom said. "I don't like it. It makes me nervous when he does that."

"Oh, Mom!" Rick waved away her words with his hand. "Don't be so nervous. Mr. Schwartz has been flying airplanes for a long time."

Mom didn't seem impressed with Mr. Schwartz's expertise. She was still shaking her head in disapproval as she went down the stairs. As the sound of the airplane faded, there was a knock at the door. It was Carlie. Mom gave her some last-minute instructions and headed out to the car with keys in her hand. "Be good," she called, before driving away. Carlie let Chris and Laurie wave goodbye to Mom before closing the door.

Carlie turned around to see her brother and Rick. They'd just put a box on the living room floor.

"Ask her," Rick said, nudging Marcus.

"No, you ask her," Marcus said.

"She's *your* sister."

"Which is exactly why *you* should ask her. She'll definitely tell me no."

"Ask me what?" Carlie said, propping Laurie on one hip and taking Chris's hand.

Rick cleared his throat. "Will you watch our puppies while we take Tim out to the airport? The puppies just ate, and they're sleeping, so they probably won't even wake up for a while."

"Puppies?" Carlie peeked over the edge of the box and bent down on one knee. "What do you feed them?"

"We checked the Internet for how to make puppy formula," Rick said. "It's kind of nasty, but they love it!"

"Oh, wook at the cutesy-wootsie wittle puppy wuppies. Sweetie peetie goosey woosey wumple snumpagins."

Rick and Marcus stared at each other is disbelief as Carlie talked to the pile of sleeping puppies.

"Snuggle wuggle fuzzy wuzzy wittle faces. Sweepy wittle punkin puppies, I could just kiss a wittle nosey wosey."

Rick hesitated for a moment. "Uh, is that a 'yes?'" he asked finally. "You'll watch them?"

"Of course!" Carlie said. She didn't even look their way. "Der wittle paws is so kute, and a wittle faces so sweet, and a wittle ears taking a nap, I will watch over sleepy baby puppy wuppies."

"Ooooh . . . K," Rick said slowly, as he and Marcus backed out the front door with Tim in tow.

"Your sister is kind of weird," Tim announced to Marcus as they walked down the path into the woods.

"Tell me something I don't know, man," Marcus said. "I have experienced her weirdness to the maximum degree. I have to live with her."

"Well, at least she's babysitting the puppy wuppies for us," Rick giggled.

"Yeah, the goosey woosey wumple snumpagins," Tim added, and then screamed in laughter as Marcus pretended to chase him through the woods.

The boys walked across the field to where the P-51 Mustang was parked near the airport hangar. Sunlight sparkled off its body and wings.

Mr. Schwartz came around one wing and waved at the boys. "I'm leaving soon. You stay and watch me take off, yah?" He smiled at Rick, who nodded excitedly. "I come back this evening. It's nice day for flying."

The boys hung around while Mr. Schwartz talked with Jim and Rob. Before long, he climbed into his P-51 Mustang and saluted the boys as he taxied toward the short stretch of runway. The P-51 Mustang gained speed and lifted off the ground. A few seconds later, Mr. Schwartz circled and came back, storming a few feet above the hangar while the boys covered their ears and grinned wildly. This time, the plane became a small dot in the blue sky that soon disappeared into the distance.

"Crazy bird," Jim muttered, staring after him. "He lives for the thrill, that's for sure."

"So how have you been?" Rob asked Rick, wiping his hands on a rag and tossing it back so that it rested on his shoulder. "Haven't seen you around much lately."

"I've been doing fine," Rick said. "But now I have a paper route, and six puppies to take care of. Plus we're doing a lot of trumpet practice for a talent show, so I haven't had time to do much else."

"Well, in a few weeks, Rob and I are going to do something that might interest you." Jim's eyes danced with suspense. "We're going to rebuild another airplane." He paused for effect. "A Super Cub, to be exact."

Rick's heart almost jumped out of his chest. "Can I come watch?" he begged.

"Watch?" Rob laughed. "Of course you can. We'll even let you help."

"That is so awesome, guys. Thanks." Rick was amazed at his good fortune.

Marcus and Tim had wandered back toward the

woods, so Rick reluctantly said goodbye to Jim and Rob and started after them.

"We'll let you know when we start on that Super Cub," Rob promised as Rick waved. He dragged his feet as he headed toward the boys. There was no place he'd rather be than the airport. Oh, well, he had to catch up with his little brother. He threw a last look at the airfield then took off at a trot.

"Hey, where are you guys going?" Rick said, out of breath when he caught up with them. They'd stopped, and Marcus was pointing to the tree line.

"Look," he said. "There's something strange going on. See the smoke coming from the woods?"

"Is it a fire?" Rick asked curiously. "Let's go check it out."

The boys ran through the woods toward the smoke they could see drifting above the trees. Sure enough, someone had started a small fire in the woods. With every second another dry leaf was ignited, and the fire was spreading before their eyes.

"Look—matches!" Tim said, picking up a half-used book of matches from the ground.

"Somebody started this fire on purpose!" Marcus shouted. "We've got to call the fire department."

"By the time we get home, call the fire department, and the fire trucks come the whole woods will be on fire," Rick said. "Maybe we can stamp it out before it gets too big."

Rick commanded Tim to stay back while he and

Marcus stamped and kicked dirt over the flames. By the time the last flame had been extinguished, both boys were sweaty and covered in black soot.

"Who would start a fire like this and just leave it?" Rick asked, shaking his head at the thought of being so stupid. "Think of all the houses and people that live right over that hill."

With his toe, Marcus traced a pattern through the leaves on the ground. "Maybe someone named Ben who doesn't like where he lives?"

"Look what else I found," Tim said, leading Rick to the bushes. "A bike."

Sure enough, a nice BMX bike had been hidden in the bushes, camouflaged with branches and leaves.

"This is too weird. A person wouldn't come out here, light a fire, and then leave matches *and* their bicycle as evidence," Marcus said. "That doesn't make sense."

A new thought dawned on Rick. "Maybe it's stolen."

Without even talking about it, they pulled the branches back and wheeled the bike back onto the path.

"It's a cool bike," Marcus said.

"Yeah," Rick agreed. "Bikes like these cost a lot of money. Let's go show it to my dad when he gets home."

Rick pushed it home while Marcus and Tim followed. He propped it up in the garage, and they all went inside.

"Stop right there," Mom commanded from the kitchen where she was putting away groceries. "Why in the world are you covered in soot?"

"Somebody lit a fire in the woods, and Rick and Marcus got it to go out before it burned the house down," Tim said. "And we found a bike."

Mom looked alarmed. "Who lit a fire in the woods?"

"We don't know," Rick said. "It was already going when we got there, and whoever started it was gone."

"What's this about a bike?" Dad had come in behind them in time to hear Tim's story.

"There was a bike in the bushes," Marcus explained. "There was no one around, and we think it might have been stolen, because someone tried to hide it there."

The boys showed Dad the bike, and he nodded. "You're right," he said. "That's strange. I think we'd better call the police in case someone reported it stolen. They also need to know about the fire."

"If no one claims the bike, can we keep it?" Rick asked.

"I think so," Dad said. "But we'll have to see what the police officer says, and we want to do our best to get it to its rightful owner."

"Maybe there will be a reward for finding it," Marcus suggested.

A half hour later, a city police car pulled up next to the driveway, and two uniformed officers knocked on the front door. Rick and Marcus watched as Dad took them into the garage to show them the bike. "If you don't mind, we'd like to have a word with your boys," one of the officers said.

"Of course," Dad said.

The police officers talked with each of the boys separately, and asked each of them to tell the story of what happened. As the officers asked question after question, a horrible thought occurred to Rick. What if the officers suspected them of stealing the bike and starting the fire? Rick cringed when he saw Tim pull the book of matches from his pocket to show them. That made them look even guiltier. He waited nervously while the officers asked their questions of each person, and then brought them all back together.

"We've been having a lot of trouble in this neighborhood lately," one of the officers said sternly. "Fortunately, you boys had your story straight, because you all told us the same thing. But we *will* find out who is doing all of this; you can be sure of that."

The officers put the bike in the trunk of their car and drove away down the street.

The boys were somber as they looked at each other. "Dad," Rick said, "I think they suspected *us*."

"Don't feel badly, son," Dad said. "By asking all of those questions, they were doing their job. You told them the truth, and that was the most important thing." He put a hand on Marcus' shoulder. "You guys had quite an adventure today. Adventures almost seem to be following your around."

"It'll have to follow me home then," Marcus said. "Mom'll send Carlie after me if I'm not home pretty soon." He turned to Rick with a grin. "See you tomorrow."

Marcus walked down the street toward his house. As if on cue, Ben came out with his basketball and started shooting some hoops. Dad and Tim went back inside, but Rick walked across the street to Ben.

"What happened to you?" Ben asked, looking at Rick's sooty face and clothes.

"Somebody started a fire in the woods."

"Well, that was pretty stupid," Ben muttered, aiming his shot.

"Yeah, I thought so, too," Rick said, watching Ben carefully for a reaction. "We had to put it out before it burned down the whole neighborhood. And we found a stolen bike. We reported it to the police."

Ben threw his basketball into the garage and turned to look at Rick. "Let me guess, then you leaped over tall buildings in a single bound and—what else—oh, you moved faster than a speeding bullet. Why are you telling me all of this? You think you're some kind of superhero, don't you? Living over there with your happy little family in your perfect little world." His voice broke. "Why don't you just leave me alone?" he shouted, then spinning around he stomped back into his house and slammed the door.

Rick shrugged. "Whatever," he mumbled as he headed back across the street. He took a long shower before dinner. Ben hadn't acted guilty, but maybe he was just a good liar. It was awfully coincidental that all of these things started happening as soon as Ben moved here. At any rate, Rick knew that eventually everything would come out. After all, now the police were looking into it.

Rick had just sat down for dinner, when the windows began to rattle.

"It's that Mr. Schwartz again," Mom said, looking exasperated. "He's going to make dinner rattle right off the table with that airplane of his."

Rick watched the light fixture above him swinging slightly with the vibration as he listened to the P-51 Mustang storm overhead. It seemed even closer than before. He closed his eyes, listening intently. It sounded different this time—as if something was wrong. A slight tremble of fear gripped him, and he thought about all the times his mom prayed for their protection, and for the protection of the pilots who landed airplanes in the airport behind their house.

Suddenly, there was a deafening sound, like a crack of thunder, followed by the screeching of metal. Mom jumped up from the table and covered her ears, and Chris and Laurie started to cry. Rick looked out the back window, over the woods toward the airport, a sick feeling rising in the pit of his stomach. He'd known what had happened in a heartbeat. Mr. Schwartz had crashed the P-51 Mustang.

Chapter 11

In a matter of seconds, Dad had his shoes on and was headed out the door. Rick and Tim were right on his heels.

"Be careful!" Mom called after them.

The door slammed shut, and the three of them ran down toward the woods. By the time they reached the last stand of trees, Rick's burning lungs felt like they were about to burst. He slowed down a little—he *had* to—and turned to his brother. "Come on, Tim."

"I'm coming," Tim shouted, closing in on Rick.

Together they followed Dad through the trees and into the clearing. Already, fire trucks had pulled onto the scene, and firefighters and paramedics poured out of the vehicles.

Rick blinked and stared at what remained of the P-51 Mustang. It had finally come to a stop just a few feet from the airplane hangar. Crushed beneath it was something that could have been a station wagon. Rick looked at the twisted metal of the airplane's nose and wondered if Mr. Schwartz could still be alive. His eyes scanned the runway and airfield, the flashing lights and emergency personnel. He was looking for Jim and Rob, but he didn't see them anywhere. Rick looked down at his feet and saw the propeller of the P-51 Mustang on the ground. *It must have been sheared off during the crash,* he thought.

Just then Rick became aware that he could smell the fuel that had sprayed out onto the runway, and so he pulled Tim back several feet.

"If that plane ignites, the spilled fuel will ignite too," Rick told his little brother. "So stay back."

"Good thinking, Rick," Dad said.

Just then, one of the neighbors walked over to where the three of them stood. "Did you see what happened?" Dad asked.

"Yes," the man said. "It was unbelievable. The plane came in a little sideways and the tip of a wing caught the ground. It cart-wheeled all the way down the runway. Then it screeched and crashed into those people in that car."

"There are *people* in that car?" Rick said in disbelief. The top of the car was smashed down on top of the door handles. Rick felt sick as he thought of the people who'd probably been crushed inside.

"Yes, and they're still in the car," the neighbor said. "What's left of them, I guess. The most amazing thing is, the pilot's fine. He was thrown from the plane when it crashed, but he only has minor injuries."

There didn't seem anything else to say. Dad just shook his head, putting a hand on both of his sons.

Before long a rescue team arrived at the car. Rick stood and watched with his dad and Tim as they worked to cut through the crunched metal so they could free the people trapped inside. It was astounding, but the trapped people were talking. It took more than an hour for the team to remove a slice of the car and pull each victim from the wreckage. The bystanders watched in amazement as each person climbed out of the mangled vehicle still buried under the plane, and stood to the side. Not one of them seemed to be seriously injured.

"It's a miracle. It's just a miracle," Dad kept saying.

Just then Rick saw Rob and Jim, sitting off to the side. Both of them looked dazed, and both held bags of ice on their heads.

"Dad, can I go talk to Rob and Jim?" Rick asked. "I'll stay out of the way of the rescue crews."

Dad thought for a minute as he looked around. "All right," he said. "Just be careful."

"Hey," Rick said breathlessly when he got to the men. "Are you guys hurt?"

Rob looked at Jim before answering. "Just got knocked unconscious for a few minutes, is all."

Jim grimaced and moved the ice bag slightly to the left side of his forehead.

"Both of you?" Rick asked. "What happened?"

Rob snorted. "Well, as far as I can remember, we both looked down the runway and saw the P-51 Mustang galloping toward the hangar. Jim here headed to the left to get out of its way, and I headed to the right to get out of its way, and—"

"We ran into each other and cracked heads," Jim finished with a wry laugh.

"Ow!" Rick said, his own head aching at the thought. "You two may be more injured than the ones involved in the crash."

"Ironic, isn't it?" Rob said, looking grumpily at Jim.

"Maybe what we need is a well-thought-out evacuation route," Jim said. "Instead of running willy-nilly every which way anytime there's an emergency."

"Maybe now that Schwartz doesn't have a plane to terrorize the neighborhood with anymore, we don't need an evacuation route," Rob countered.

Rick could tell by the way they bantered back and forth that they were going to be just fine. He said goodbye, and headed toward his dad and Tim.

When they got home, they took turns telling Mom and Chris and Laurie about the plane crash, and how everyone survived. Mom was amazed and thankful, and had tears in her eyes when they told her about the people being pulled from the car, unhurt.

"That is the most incredible thing I've heard in a long time," Mom said quietly. "What a miracle."

Rick thought again about all of the times Mom had prayed for the pilots who took off and landed at the airport behind their house. He was sure her prayers had everything to do with the fact that no one was killed. That night, as they prayed during their family worship, he paid more attention to the words he prayed. Now, more than ever, he realized the power of prayer.

Chapter 12

A week later, the excitement of the plane crash had died down and life in Rick's neighborhood was almost back to normal. The puppies were getting livelier, and a few of them had figured out how to climb out of the box. They'd topple down onto the floor, then toddle around, exploring. Rick knew it wouldn't be long until the rest of the puppies figured out the secret to escaping their cardboard crib, and soon there'd be puppies going in every direction.

"Let's take them outside to play in the grass," Marcus said one day, scratching a little white and black one behind the ear.

"Ouch." Rick laughed as Little Lamb's sharp little teeth gnawed on the end of his finger. "Yeah, let's take them outside."

Rick and Marcus watched the puppies carefully as they teetered through the new terrain. They hadn't been outside long, when Ben's mom appeared on the sidewalk.

"What cute puppies," she said, bending down to get a closer look. "Where did you get them?"

"Someone left them on our doorstep a few weeks ago," Rick replied. "We've been feeding them and taking care of them because they don't have a mother."

"Oh, that's sad." Ben's mom frowned. "I can't believe someone just left them on your doorstep. But you guys are doing a great job. Look at them. They all seem healthy and strong. Are you going to keep them all?"

Rick shook his head. "No, we have to find homes for them as soon as they're old enough. We're going to sell them to raise money for a mission plane. Mom said she thinks they'll be ready in about a week or so."

Ben's mom looked thoughtful as she watched the puppies play. "I'd like to buy one from you when they're ready," she said. "For Ben. He's been so lonely and sad since his dad died."

Rick looked up in surprise. "His dad—died?"

Ben's mom nodded. "Yes, and I had to take a job to support us. That's why we moved here. I got a job with the newspaper, which was good, but Ben not only lost his dad and the home he grew up in, but all of his friends at the same time. He's having a hard time adjusting." She stopped and took a deep breath. "I think we both are."

"I'm sorry," Rick mumbled, not sure what to say.

"So am I," Ben's mom said sadly. "But I've noticed how you two have tried to be nice and include him. I surely appreciate it, even though I know he hasn't been receptive. I just hope you don't give up.

Somewhere behind all of that anger and sadness is a pretty great kid."

Rick looked at Marcus, whose eyes were as big as dinner plates.

There were tears in Ben's mom's eyes when she stood up. "Anyway, if it's OK, I'd like to place an order for a puppy. Let me know when it's time, and I'll bring Ben over to pick one out."

"Sounds good," Rick said. "Of course we'll let you know."

"Also, I know a woman who writes a column for the newspaper on stories such as your puppy rescue. Maybe she'll want to come down and write a piece about you and the puppies. You could get your picture in the paper."

"That would be great!" Rick exclaimed, excited at the thought of being in the newspaper. Marcus looked excited, too, and smiled widely as he corralled the frisky puppies on the lawn.

"Can you believe it?" Marcus asked when Ben's mom left.

"I know. It's amazing." Rick picked up the puppies one by one and put them back in the box. "We might be in the newspaper."

"That's not what I meant," Marcus continued quietly. "I mean about Ben."

"Oh, yeah." Rick paused. "Well, now we know why he's been such a jerk."

"I might be a jerk too if that happened to me."

Marcus stood up and helped Rick lift the box of puppies to carry back into the house. "I guess Ben needs us to be his friends, whether he likes it or not."

"So let's not give up," Rick huffed as he and Marcus gently lowered the box to the floor. "Let's keep Operation Fiery Coals in effect until it works."

Just then they heard a squeal of brakes and saw their mail carrier pulling up to their mailbox. Rick sprinted outside, hurrying back into the house with an armful of mail. Under the usual stack of bills and junk mail was a new flight magazine.

"Look," Rick said, holding the magazine out to Marcus. "It's the glider issue. It says there are instructions inside to build your own glider."

The boys poured some lemonade, and went out on the back porch with the new magazine. After situating themselves in lawn chairs, they began reading the article on glider construction.

"Hey, we have some of these materials already," Rick told Marcus, going down the list with his index finger. "Remember that old parachute I bought when we went with my dad to the Army surplus store? We could use that for the nylon."

"Yeah, good idea," Marcus said. "That's perfect."

"But where are we going to find aluminum piping?" Rick massaged his forehead with his right hand as he thought.

"Are you kidding?" Marcus laughed. "My dad is an electrician. Don't you remember what my garage looks like? We have aluminum conduit coming out of our ears."

Rick looked up in amazement. "That's right!" he said excitedly. "What was I thinking?"

"But we can't fly to South America on a hang glider." Marcus had a sensible look on his face. "Where would we put the supplies?"

"No," Rick laughed. "That's not what the hang glider's for. Do you know how much these things sell for? We could probably get a couple thousand for it, easy."

"Oh? Build it and sell it." Marcus nodded. "Well, what are we waiting for? Let's build it in my garage—there's lots of room, and if we put it together there, then we don't have to haul the aluminum piping anywhere."

"Let me go get my parachute," Rick said. "Oh, and do you think we should keep this our secret? You know, until after the test flight is done and everything, so it will be a surprise?"

Marcus agreed. "Not only that, but anyone who'd want to sabotage our project wouldn't even know about it."

"Know about what?" Tim asked, coming around the corner.

Rick took a deep breath and then let the air out slowly through his lips. "Listen, I can't tell you right now, because it's a secret. But we need you to play with the puppies until we get back, and watch to make sure they don't get out of the box. It's very important. Can you do that for us?"

Tim nodded. "But when can I know the secret?"

"Soon," Rick promised. "It's going to be big, and it's going to make us a lot of money for our Super Cub. Be patient, OK? And don't tell anyone."

Tim was agreeable and went back inside the house to the puppy box. Rick pulled the parachute out of his dad's garage, and they walked down the street to Marcus's house. Before long, the boys had compiled all of the necessary materials and cut the nylon parachute into huge strips, just as the instructions directed.

"Wait a minute," Rick said suddenly. "There's one thing we didn't think about. How are we going to sew all of these strips back together in the correct formation?"

Marcus made a face and scratched his cheek. "Good question."

"What are you guys doing in here?" Carlie's voice echoed in the garage as the inside door swung open. "You've made a huge mess."

Rick almost jumped out of his skin. "You scared me," he grumbled.

"I scared *you?*" Carlie demanded, her hands on her hips. "I heard noises coming from the garage and thought we had an intruder or something. What *are* you doing?"

"Can you keep a secret?" Rick asked.

"Rick!" Marcus gave him a look.

Rick put out a hand as if to tell Marcus to wait.

Carlie looked suspicious. "Yeah, what is it?"

"Don't you have a sewing machine?" Rick asked.

"Yeah." Carlie waited.

"Well," Rick bargained, "we'll tell you the secret if you'll sew these strips together for us."

Carlie thought for a minute. "OK, I guess. I don't have anything else to do."

When Rick and Marcus explained the hang glider idea to Carlie, she shrugged. "That's your big secret?"

A couple of hours later, all of the strips had been sewn into one piece. It was just the right size to fit over the frame.

"I've got to go," Rick said, noticing the pink shades of sunset in the sky as he looked out the window. "We'll have to start working on the frame tomorrow. My mom's going to wonder where I am." He pointed a finger at Carlie. "Remember, this is a secret. Don't tell anyone, OK?"

"OK," Carlie answered. "Sure."

Rick helped Marcus pick up all of the supplies and put them in the corner out of the way, and then he ran down the street toward home.

Chapter 13

"Hey, Mom?" Rick called from the front door. "I'm going over to Marcus's house, OK?"

Rick had hardly slept the night before, with all the excitement from their hang glider experiment. When the alarm went off he wasn't sure that he'd slept at all. It showed, too, when they did their paper route. He accidentally tossed Mr. Smith's paper into the dog's water dish on the front porch, and the couple in the gray house down the street now had a newspaper on their roof. It was a good thing the newspaper company gave them extra papers in case of an accident—this morning he'd had two!

"Sorry, you're not going anywhere," Mom said as she walked into the living room, drying her hands on a towel. "Right after lunch, I had a call from the newspaper reporter that Ben's mom talked with about your puppy story. She's coming over to interview you. In fact, I just got off of the phone with Carlie, and she's sending Marcus over here too."

Tim came downstairs in a suit and tie, and his church shoes on his feet. He had put gel in his hair, and every strand was perfectly in place. He would have looked like one of those model kids in a magazine if it hadn't been for the grape jelly on his face.

"What are you doing?" Rick laughed.

"I'm looking good for the newspaper," Tim said defensively.

"It wouldn't hurt for *you* to go change into some nicer clothes and comb your hair," Mom chided Rick as she rubbed the jelly off of Tim's cheek.

When the reporter rang the doorbell, the boys had the puppies ready. Rick suspected that Tim had put gel in the puppies' hair, too, but he couldn't be sure.

The reporter was pretty and young and excited to see the puppies. She asked the boys a lot of questions about the puppies and about the mission plane they were hoping to buy, and she wrote in her notebook when they answered. She held each one of the puppies separately, cooing at their little faces, and took several pictures of them with the boys.

"You guys have done an amazing job with these puppies," the reporter told them. "I'll bet when this article comes out, you'll have lots of people wanting to give them good homes. Are all of them leaving, or are you keeping any?"

Rick swallowed and felt a pang in his chest as he looked at Little Lamb, who was just figuring out how to wag his tail. "I guess we have to sell them all," he mumbled. "Dad's not a big puppy person."

The reporter followed his gaze to the little white

puppy and smiled at Rick. "Well, it's none of my business," she said softly as though she was telling him a secret, "but I think you've proven yourself to be a responsible guy. I mean, if you can raise and feed six puppies, taking care of one should be no big deal, right?"

Rick nodded and blushed when she winked at him.

The reporter promised that their story would be in the newspaper within the week, and praised them all again for their hard work before she got into her car and drove away. When she had gone, Tim looked up at Rick and grinned. "Rick wants to marry the newspaper girl, Rick wants to marry the newspaper girl," he chanted.

"I do not." Rick could feel his face turning red, and he looked at Marcus to help him out.

Marcus shook his head. "Sorry, man. I have to agree with your little brother. When she called you a 'responsible guy,' I thought you were going to float up to the ceiling."

"Rick wants to marry the newspaper girl," Tim shouted, his enthusiasm fueled by Marcus's agreement.

Rick tried to ignore Tim's chanting, and gave Marcus a meaningful look. "Don't we have a *project* to work on?"

"Yeah," Marcus grinned. "If you can keep your mind on the task at hand."

Rick commissioned Tim to watch over the puppies, and told his mom he was going to be at Marcus's house all afternoon.

Marcus's parents weren't home, but Carlie was there chatting away on the telephone. She waved at them when they came in. "I'm baking some cookies. You guys can have some when they're ready," she called.

"Your sister's not so bad," Rick said as he closed the door between the living room and the garage. "She's actually kind of cool. She watched our puppies, and sewed our nylon strips together, and now she's baking cookies for us."

Marcus nodded and picked up a piece of metal piping. "Yeah, I know. She's a pretty good sister," he admitted. "Don't get too excited about the cookies, though. She's not much of a cook. I've learned to take only one and smile politely, even if it tastes like cement. Just chew softly, so you don't break any teeth."

"Point taken," Rick laughed as he picked up the magazine and thumbed through to the hang glider instructions.

It took them three afternoons to configure all of the metal pieces, and decide which fittings to use and where to use them. The pieces came together, and slowly, a hang glider frame took shape before their eyes. When the segments were all securely in place, they stretched the nylon tightly over the frame, and attached all of the edges. At last they were finally finished. Rick and Marcus stood back to take a look at the results of their work.

Rick almost felt patriotic as he looked at the beautiful wingspan of the hang glider, gleaming there in the stream of sunlight that came through the garage window.

"It looks just like the picture." Marcus whistled in admiration. "Are we good or what?"

Rick sat down on the garage floor and wiped his sweaty hair out of his face. "Well, we won't know for sure until we take it out on a test flight. But right now, I'd say we're good to go."

Rick and Marcus discussed all of the potential test flight sites, finally settling on a sharp embankment overlooking the Auburn valley. It was on the other side of the airport. The area was isolated so they wouldn't attract a lot of attention, and the drop off was steep enough that they were sure to catch a draft to aid their flight.

"This is heavy," Marcus grunted as he and Rick lifted the hang glider and tried to walk carrying it. "It's going to take us forever to get it to the launch site."

"Stop thinking about it," Rick commanded, shifting his shoulder slightly to get a better position under its weight. "The more you think about it, the heavier it will seem."

The hang glider transport became tricky in the woods when they had to maneuver the large wingspan through the trees. When they finally crossed the airport runway, trekked through another stretch of woods, and reached the embankment, both Rick and Marcus were exhausted. They surveyed the drop off and their intended flight path across the valley.

"As long as we clear the gravel pit to the west," Rick said, "we should be able to fly all the way into the downtown area and land in a large parking lot somewhere, don't you think?"

Marcus squinted across the valley and nodded. "Yeah. Good thinking."

"And," Rick added, "maybe after we land, we should call that newspaper reporter, and see if she wants to write a column on our flight."

Marcus looked at Rick with a triumphant gleam in his eye. "Tim was right," he sang out. "Rick wants to marry the newspaper girl."

"Show a little maturity, please," Rick said, wishing he'd never mentioned the reporter. "I was suggesting that this might be a newsworthy event, and—oh, never mind. Which one of us is actually going to do the test flight?"

"Good question," Marcus pondered. "I guess whichever of us is the lightest."

"We weigh about the same," Rick reminded him.

They sat in silence for a minute while they tried to decide.

"I guess we could toss a coin," Rick suggested.

"Hmmm." Marcus looked at Rick. "What about Tim?"

"What about him?"

"He's the lightest. And if we showed him how, he could steer it. It's not that complicated."

"Marcus, you are a genius." Rick stood up and

dusted off the back of his jeans. "Let's go get him."

"No," Marcus shook his head. "I'll stay here and make sure no one tries to steal the hang glider or sabotage our flight. You go get Tim."

When Rick got home he found Tim trying to teach the puppies how to do tricks.

"Watch," Tim said excitedly, pointing to the littlest black one. "I told that one to fall over, and he did."

"Tim, about all they *can* do at this point is fall over," Rick reminded him.

"No, he obeyed me," Tim said. "Watch this. Go to sleep." he commanded the black and white one who was sleeping in the corner of the box. Tim looked up at Rick victoriously. "See?"

Rick shook his head. "OK, whatever. Listen, you know the secret project that Marcus and I have been working on?"

Tim nodded.

"Well," Rick continued. "It's time to let you in on it. In fact, you get to have a very important part in it."

"What is it?" Tim asked, getting up from the puppy box and brushing his hands on his pants.

"You'll see," Rick said as Tim followed him to the garage. "I'll take you to where it is. Bring your football helmet."

Tim stopped walking. "Why do I need my football helmet?" he asked suspiciously.

"It's for just in case," Rick said. "You'll be fine, I

promise. I'll explain everything when we get there." Rick stopped and thought for a moment. "And, uh, bring your skateboard pads, too. For just in case."

When they arrived at the embankment, Rick and Marcus helped Tim get ready for the test flight. Tim looked twice as big with his helmet and all of his pads on, and he could hardly contain his excitement when he saw the hang glider. "This is what you've been working on? You guys built this?" he asked in wonderment.

"Yep, and you are going to be the star," Marcus said. "Because you get to be the one to fly it."

"Fly it?" Tim asked, astonishment crossing his face.

Marcus looked at Rick. "You didn't tell him?"

"I was getting to that," Rick said, giving Marcus a grumpy look. "Now, Tim, you get to fly it, because you're the lightest one."

Rick and Marcus strapped him in, and showed Tim how to use the bar for steering, and which direction he should go when the hang glider took flight. At the last minute Rick put some change in Tim's pocket.

"When you land downtown, call us from a payphone, and we'll have Mom or Carlie come and pick you up in the car," Rick told him. "Maybe you can even be in the newspaper again."

Standing on the edge of the embankment, looking down, Tim didn't look too sure of the plan. But he did seem excited at having such an important role to play.

"Now all we have to do is wait for wind," Rick said.

The three of them stood on the edge of the drop-off, waiting. Several minutes passed, but nothing happened. Rick licked his finger and held it up in the air. Not even a slight breeze.

"Well, this is great," Marcus said.

"Are you sure this thing is going to fly?" Tim asked, grunting under the weight of the hang glider. "It's awfully heavy."

"Of course," Rick said, irritated. "We made it exactly like the instructions said."

They waited for a little longer, but no wind came. All three of them were starting to feel restless.

"All right," Rick said finally. "Let's do this. Let's back Tim up with the hang glider, and let him get a running start. Once he gets in the air, he'll have lift."

The older boys helped Tim inch backwards until he was a good running distance from the drop off.

"Are you ready?" Rick asked Tim.

"I guess so," Tim replied.

At the count of three, Tim started running. Rick and Marcus ran along beside him, supporting the wings of the hang glider until they reached the edge of the drop-off. Rick and Marcus stopped, and Tim sailed off of the embankment. The hang glider flew through the air as Rick and Marcus watched in elation.

For about three seconds.

Suddenly, gravity overcame the glider's heavy frame. It dropped straight down the embankment, tumbling over itself down the hill until it crashed to a stop at the bottom. Rick and Marcus stared in horror. All they could see of Tim was a small foot poking out from under the tip of one of the wings. Panicked, Rick took a flying leap.

"Oh, please, God," he prayed out loud as he half fell, half slid down the steep incline. "Please let my little brother be OK. I'll never do anything this stupid again. Just please let him be all right."

Tears stung Rick's eyes as he reached the hang glider and slightly lifted one wing. Underneath the crumpled mass of bent metal and torn nylon he saw a motionless little figure wearing a football helmet.

Chapter 14

"T im? Tim, are you OK?" Rick gasped. "I'm so sorry. Please say something."

Rick looked back up the hill at Marcus, who still stared, terrified, at the hang glider.

"Say something," Rick begged, looking under the broken wing at his little brother.

"Get this thing off of me," Tim shouted, his voice muffled by the football helmet.

Rick laughed in relief. "OK, buddy, hold on!" he said, crying and laughing at the same time.

"Get down here and help me get this thing off of him," he shouted up to Marcus.

Marcus stumbled down the hill and helped Rick lift the bent metal and nylon wings off of Tim, who climbed out from under it all in a pretty lousy mood.

"Followed the instructions, huh?" Tim yelled, pulling off his football helmet and pointing to the crashed glider. "Maybe you guys should stick to paper airplanes. Did you ever think about that? I changed my mind. I don't want to fly in your Super Cub. I'd rather live."

Rick was happy to see that Tim was unhurt, and didn't mind his outburst. "Climb on my back. I'll carry you home," he said.

Tim was about to refuse, but changed his mind as he looked up the hill. Grudgingly, he climbed onto Rick's back. By the time they reached home, Rick was seriously exhausted, but Tim was in much better spirits.

"It's a good thing I had on my skateboard pads," Tim said cheerfully. "And my football helmet. When I was flying, it was so cool—for like one second—and then all of a sudden, the ground was coming up really fast. And I almost died."

Mom was folding clothes when they walked in. She stopped mid-fold and stared at them with her mouth open. "Where have you been?" she demanded. "And what in the world happened? And what have you done to your little brother?" Her voice grew louder with each question as she looked at their dirt-caked jeans, Tim's dented football helmet, and his scraped skateboard pads.

Tim took a deep breath as Rick lowered him off of his back. "Rick and Marcus built this really big—"

Rick clamped a hand over Tim's mouth before he could continue. "I'll tell this one," he said quietly. Tim's mouth shut. He looked up at Rick. Rick took a deep breath of his own.

"Marcus and I built a hang glider," Rick began. "In Marcus' garage, using the instructions from my flight magazine. We took it over to the embankment on the other side of the airport and decided that Tim should do the test flight, since he's lighter . . ." Rick swallowed as he saw the look on his mother's face. "But he crashed at the bottom of the hill."

"How could you *do* something like that?" Mom asked, her voice choked with panic. "He could have been seriously injured—and—or—"

"Died?" Tim suggested.

"Tim, you're not helping," Rick whispered loudly.

Mom came over and grabbed Tim, looking him over from head to toe.

Rick's chest was heavy, and he wished he could disappear altogether.

"I'm sorry, Mom. It was really stupid. I never meant for him to get hurt," Rick explained, his words rushing out without his taking a breath. "I really thought it would work." Tears misted his eyes. "I don't even care what punishment I get. I was so afraid that he was hurt. I'm just glad he's OK."

"No," Marcus said. He seemed to stand a little taller. "It's my fault, Mrs. Bockmann. It was my idea to use Tim, because he was the lightest. I'm sorry."

Rick's mom didn't say anything, but her hands were shaking as she hugged Tim closely.

Tim took his mom's face in his hands and held it up so that he could look into her eyes. "I'm all right, Mom. I didn't have any injuries. And they didn't make me do it. I wanted to."

Mom took a ragged breath. "Well, everyone's OK, and right now, that's the important thing. You guys get cleaned up for dinner. Your dad will be home soon, and we'll talk later."

Marcus went home, while Rick and Tim took off their dusty shoes and trudged up the stairs.

~ ~ ~

The next morning, Rick felt a little better. Tim had forgiven him, and he'd had a chance to explain to his parents what happened, including how he felt after the crash and what he'd learned. Rick promised to clean up the hang glider wreckage, and to his relief, the discussion was over.

Rick and Tim delivered the last of their newspapers, and took the extras inside. "Are we in this one?" Tim asked excitedly as Mom turned a page.

"Yes," Mom announced. "Here you are."

Rick and Tim listened while Mom read the article aloud and showed them the picture.

Rick smiled as he looked at the picture of himself holding Little Lamb. He was standing next to Tim and Marcus.

"You're not the only ones who made the newspaper," Mom said with a frown, looking on the opposite page. "It looks like the police finally found out who has been committing all of the vandalism and theft going on around here."

Rick swallowed a bite of toast as a feeling of dread came over him. After everything he'd learned about Ben he was hoping that he and Marcus could have another chance to befriend him. Now it looked like it was too late.

"Hmmm," Mom said as she read on. "It was some older kids from another neighborhood. The police traced their activity and caught them."

Rick looked up. "Are they sure they found the real culprits?"

Mom nodded. "Yep. Says here they actually caught them in the act, then matched their fingerprints to stolen items and areas that had been vandalized. They're sure. Why?"

Rick was quiet. "So it wasn't Ben after all," he muttered to himself.

"What did you say?" Mom asked.

"Nothing," Rick said. "Just talking to myself."

"Well," Mom said, folding the newspaper closed, "tonight is the community talent show. You and Tim should spend some time with your trumpets today."

There was a knock at the door, and when Rick answered it, he was surprised to see Ben and his mom.

"Hi," Ben's mom said. "Your mom told us that the puppies are old enough for their new homes. Can we come in and take a look?"

Rick nodded and pulled the door open wider for them to come inside.

Ben looked uncomfortable. "Hi," he said finally.

"Hi," Rick answered. "Come on in. My mom's in the kitchen. I'll take Ben to see the puppies."

Ben followed Rick into the utility room where the puppies were yapping and playing with each other. Ben knelt down by the box. Rick thought he actually saw Ben smile as he looked at the chubby babies tumbling over each other.

"They're sure cute," Ben said.

"Yeah." Rick picked up a little black one and put it gently in Ben's arms. The puppy licked his face. "I think he likes you."

Ben was quiet for a moment as he held the squirming puppy. "Look," he said slowly, "I know I've been a real jerk. It's just that, it's just been really hard, and I—"

"I know," Rick said. "Your mom told me. I'm sorry."

Ben nodded. "So, maybe we can all shoot hoops or something sometime."

Rick smiled. "Cool."

Just then the two moms came around the corner. "Have you picked out a puppy yet?" Ben's mom asked.

"Yeah," Ben said, looking at the little black puppy in his arms and smiling at Rick. "I think I like this one."

Before Ben and his mom went home, Rick's mom invited them to come to the talent show.

"What do you think, Ben? Does that sound like fun?" Ben's mom asked.

"Sure," Ben said with a shrug. "I guess I'll see you later," he said to Rick as they left.

His words weren't all that much, but they made Rick smile.

The phone rang all morning with callers who'd read the newspaper article and were interested in buying the puppies. Mom scheduled some appointments throughout the day and promised to help Rick pick good families for them.

Rick and Tim spent the morning practicing their trumpets. When they finished, they could play their piece without a single mistake.

"We're going to win," Tim said optimistically.

"Well, we'll see," Rick said cautiously. "Don't forget, there will be other people there who can play instruments, and sing, and all kinds of stuff."

"So?" Tim responded. "We're still going to win."

Rick laughed. "I hope so."

Marcus called, and Rick agreed to meet him at the hang glider site to retrieve what was left of the wreckage. It took a long time to drag all of the pieces back up the hill, past the airport, through the woods to Marcus's house. They dismantled the metal piping and stacked it in the corner. Rick peeled off the nylon and folded it into a tattered square.

While they worked, Rick told Marcus about Ben's visit that morning, and how the police had caught the real culprits.

"I feel bad that we suspected Ben," Marcus said. "But I'm glad we were nice to him."

"Yeah," Rick added. "It looks like Operation Fiery Coals might have worked."

Marcus smiled. "Well, that's cool. It's going to be fun hanging out with him, instead of spying on him."

When Rick finally got home, he was tired, and knew that they didn't have long before they'd have to leave for the talent show. When he walked in, Dad was home and dinner was ready.

"Oh, I almost forgot," Mom said, handing Rick a stack of bills. "We sold every single puppy today. Can you believe it? The newspaper article was barely out, and already they all have homes."

Rick sat down in his chair at the dinner table and looked at the wad of bills in his hand. "We sold—all of them?" he asked slowly.

Mom nodded. "I made sure they all went to excellent families who would take care of them."

Rick ate the rest of his meal in silence, then packed up his trumpet and got ready to leave for the talent show. He tried not to think about Little Lamb. "It's my own fault," he said to himself. "I never asked to keep him. I know Dad would have said no, but I could have at least asked."

The community hall was a bustle of excitement as the audience found seats and performers lined up backstage. Mom and Dad sat down with Laurie, Chris, Marcus, and Ben and his mom. Rick and Tim went backstage.

Tim's eyes were wide. "There sure are a lot of people here," he said, looking around. They seemed to be everywhere. Adults and teens were giving their voices and instruments a last warmup before the show began. There were even some other kids on the program. To Rick's dismay, his and Tim's trumpet duet was at the very end.

The boys sat and waited, listening to the different performances. Some were funny. Some were beautiful. But they got tired waiting and walked around. The area backstage was interesting. Scenery and other props from past programs were stacked here and there. Finally, the person in line ahead of them was announced and strode out to perform.

Rick felt Tim tug at his sleeve. "What?" he asked.

"I have to go to the bathroom."

"What? Now?"

Rick looked down at him in panic. "We'll be onstage in just a couple of minutes. Can't you wait?"

Tim shook his head. "No!" he said, starting to do a little dance. "I've been waiting! I have to go *now*."

"The restrooms are all the way at the other end of the auditorium," Rick tried to reason with him. "We'll never get back in time."

"Now!" Tim insisted.

Rick laid his trumpet in its case next to Tim's, and took Tim's hand. "This is going to have to be the fastest bathroom break you've ever taken."

Chapter 15

Rick and Tim sprinted through the side exit door and around to the other end of the gymnasium. Rick tapped his feet outside of the men's restroom while he waited for Tim. Just as the last performer sang her ending notes, Tim burst out through the door.

"Did you wash your—never mind," Rick said in a panic. "Let's go!"

They ran around outside the building again, and came through the backstage door just as the announcer began speaking. "And now, ladies and gentlemen—Rick and Tim Bockmann, and a trumpet duet."

Out of breath, Rick and Tim stumbled onto the stage, trumpets in hand. Blinded by the spotlight, Rick nudged Tim with his elbow. Their piece began with his trumpet. "Play," he hissed.

Tim was still breathing hard from their sprinted restroom trip, but he took a deep breath and tried to play. The sound that came out of the trumpet was like a braying donkey. *Hoooonk.*

The audience laughed. Embarrassed, Rick tried to play his trumpet. But his lungs were still on fire and all that came out was a series of toots.

Honkeeonkeeonk.

The audience roared some more, and Rick didn't know what to do. Tim and Rick each tried to start the song, several times, to no avail. Each time, their trumpets sounded like sick donkeys. Rick was ready to run offstage and hide, when Tim lifted the trumpet to his lips. At last he'd caught his breath enough to play his opening notes. Rick joined in. To Rick's relief, they finished the rest of the song, bowed, and walked offstage. The auditorium thundered with applause.

"They were laughing at us." Tim almost cried as they retreated behind the curtain. "We sounded awful!"

The other performers backstage smiled at them. Rick could almost taste their pity.

"It's OK, man, cheer up," Rick said, even though he didn't feel cheery at all. "We did our best. That was the plan, right? Who cares that we lost the prize?"

Now all they could do was wait.

Someone came on stage and did a talking routine while the votes were being counted. But finally the announcer came out onto the stage. He made a little speech about how everyone had done very well, and it was too bad that they couldn't all get awards. The third place winner is —" he announced, and everyone clapped. "Number two . . . And first prize goes to . . ."

The three performers walked onstage to collect their awards.

"Can't we go find Mom and Dad now?" Tim said miserably, snapping shut his trumpet case.

"Sure," Rick said. "Come on, let's get out of here."

"And now," said the announcer, "the audience choice award."

There was a slight pause.

"Rick and Tim Bockmann, Trumpet Duet. Come on out here, you comedians."

Rick and Tim blankly stared at each other.

"Come on out!" the announcer called.

Dazed, the boys walked out into the spotlight. The announcer handed them a check, and the audience laughed and clapped again. Rick and Tim bowed, and walked offstage to find their parents.

"I think they thought we did that on purpose," Tim laughed, holding the check in amazement.

"You guys were so funny," Ben said. "Marcus and I laughed our heads off."

"Yeah," Marcus added. "I didn't know you were going to do a comedy show."

Marcus came over to spend the night, and when they got home Dad and Mom gathered them all into the living room for worship.

"I got another letter today—from Peru," Dad said, unfolding the paper to read.

The boys listened attentively, their imaginations once again sparked by the fascinating stories within the pages of the letter. After prayer, the boys headed upstairs to get into bed.

"Listen, guys, I was thinking," Rick said slowly. "It's going to be a while before we can actually get our pilots' licenses and everything. And the missionaries, well, they need money *now*."

"I was thinking the same thing," Marcus said, shaking his head in amazement. "We should send our Super Cub money."

"Then you agree?" Rick asked. "I mean, if we give money, it's almost like we're missionaries, because we're helping the missionaries, right?"

Rick and Marcus looked at Tim, who hadn't said a word yet. "What do you think, partner?" Rick asked. "Should we send our money to South America ahead of us?"

Tim nodded, a slow smile spreading across his face.

"Then it's settled."

Tim followed as Rick and Marcus went into the living room where Dad was still sitting in his recliner.

"Dad, we want to donate the money we were saving for our Super Cub to the missionaries. We all agreed. So in the morning, we're going to go get a money order. Will you send it to them for us?"

Dad sat up in his chair and took his glasses off. "Really?" he asked. "All of it?"

The boys nodded.

"That is very honorable. I'm proud of you," Dad said. "Of course I'll send it."

Just then, Rick heard a strange noise coming from

the utility room. "What's that?" he asked, straining to hear. "It sounds like—"

Rick walked to the utility room and opened the door. There in the cardboard box, Little Lamb stood stiffly with one ear up and one ear down, trying to work up an impressive bark. Rick turned around and saw his mom and dad standing behind him, smiling.

"He's yours," Mom said with a nod.

"Mom," Rick gasped as he scooped Little Lamb up in his arms, "I thought you said you sold all of the puppies."

"I did sell them all," Mom answered. "I just neglected to mention that one of the puppy customers was your dad."

Rick hugged his dad hard. "Thanks, Dad."

Dad grinned. "You've earned him, son."

That night, while Rick rested on his pillow listening to Marcus snore, he heard the top bunk squeak and Tim leaned over the edge. "Rick?" Tim whispered.

"Yeah?" Rick answered.

"I like being your little brother."

Rick blinked in surprise, and then smiled. "I like being your big brother," he said softly. A few minutes later, Tim was fast asleep. Rick lay there in bed, staring up at the sky through the window when he heard the doorknob turn.

"Dad? Is that you?" Rick said with a yawn.

Dad tiptoed in. "What are you still doing awake?"

"I was just thinking," Rick said. "What if Jesus

comes before I get a Super Cub? Do you think I could have one in heaven?"

Rick heard Dad chuckle softly in the dark. "Maybe," Dad replied. "But I'm pretty sure a Super Cub would be the slowest thing up there."

Dad went out quietly, closing the door behind him. By the time the hall light was out, the only thing still awake was Rick's imagination.

Rick looked over at his brave young copilot and grinned. "Are you ready for takeoff, little brother?"

Tim grinned back and gave Rick a thumbs-up sign.

With a voice-activated command, Rick initiated the propulsion reactors that rumbled beneath them, and the bold team of galactic pilots launched their expedition into deep space, dodging spinning planets and glowing stars as they spiraled through Orion's belt, faster than the speed of light . . .